The Battle of Life

Rick Harris

authorHOUSE®

AuthorHouse™ UK Ltd.
500 Avebury Boulevard
Central Milton Keynes, MK9 2BE
www.authorhouse.co.uk
Phone: 08001974150

First published by AuthorHouse 3/15/2010

ISBN: 978-1-4490-3942-4 (sc)

This book is printed on acid-free paper.

HMS GANGES

Before I left school at Christmas of 1952, I had applied and passed the exams to join the Royal Navy as a Boy Telegraphist. I had already qualified at 25 wpm in Morse code as a sea cadet. I eventually received my papers and joined several other young lads at the James Watt Street recruiting offices in Birmingham, from where we were herded to the railway station for our journey to Ipswich via London. At Ipswich station, we were met by dozens of lorries, our transport to HMS *Ganges*, at Shotley on the tip of land where the rivers Orwell and Stour meet, with Harwich and Felixtowe the other side of the rivers.

There were hundreds of us from all over the country, many not realising what they were coming to. From conversations that I had later, I'm sure that some had expected to be going to a real ship. I had older friends who had already joined, so I had some idea of what to expect, but at the age of fifteen, nothing could have prepared us for what we were about to experience over the coming months.

We queued for our kit and were taken to our accommodation in what was known as the annexe; then we were introduced to our Petty Officer instructor and our two instructor boys (boys who had completed their twelve or eighteen month training and were now qualified to bully us into shape).

The accommodation was a series of large wooden huts surrounding a parade ground. The huts were very basic dormitories fitted out with about forty bunks with kit lockers between and a wash room at the end of the building.

The toilets were in a separate building about fifty yards away.

We were to spend six weeks here learning basic drills, sewing our names into every item of kit, spending one day a week in the laundry dhobeying (washing) our dirty clothes and bedding, taking each washed item for inspection to Nobby Clarke. He was in charge of the laundry, and was an unsavoury, sadistic character who seemed to love the power that he had over us and delighted in finding imaginary bits that we had missed so that he could send us back to wash it again, most times with a flick of a towel on our bare skin. Our instructor PO was very strict but fair; he had suggested that a bit of sunshine on our bodies was good for us. Unfortunately, Nobby had a different view—if we showed signs of exposure to the sun, he believed that we were idle good-for-nothings and took great pleasure in inflicting a swipe across our bare flesh with a wet towel rung out and twisted whilst we were bent over the sinks. He was letting us know verbally one time what he thought of sunbathers when our instructor came in and disputed his argument, which only made it worse for us the next time we visited.

After we had been there a week, we got our first pay; we had to queue, take off our hat, place it on the table, and call out our official number. Two half crowns were placed on it. (25pence)

After buying a packet of washing powder and a packet of cigarettes, there was next to nothing left to last the rest of the week, so I decided to give up smoking. It was no problem as I'd never really taken to it, but it was what everyone else did.

After a couple of days, a lot of the lads were running out of cigarettes and couldn't afford to buy any, so I would sell one for sixpence to be paid the next payday. After a couple of weeks, I was something of a tobacco baron, and the day before payday I could sell one for half a crown. The lads used to write home to mom for extra cash to feed their habit.

That was my second business adventure. A few years earlier, we used to scrump apples from the big house and sell them door to door, including the home from where we had scrumped them.

As I said, our instructor PO, for whom we had great respect, was strict but fair, unlike our Instructor boys who were just bullies. It seemed as though they thought their job was to make our life hell. If we were bad, we were punished; if we weren't bad, they would invent something to punish us for. Each night we would have to clean the mess for rounds and then turn in by 2045 and have lights out at 2100. They would then start to prowl, looking for an excuse to punish. A word, groan, or even a cough would be enough. "Everybody out on the end of your beds." We would stand there perfectly still whilst one of them would shout, demeaning and belittling us. After about 30 minutes, he would instruct us to turn in. Someone always muttered something under their breath, or he imagined someone did, and we were out again; this went on most nights. We were awakened at 0500 by a shout or a dustbin being beaten in the middle of the mess, and the last six out of bed were punished, dressed in full kit plus oilskin and wearing a gas mask and doubled a few times round the parade ground. We then had to wash, dress, and make our beds, i.e., fold three blankets and two sheets in a certain way that had been taught, with our names showing on the folds in line and dead centre, stacked upon each other with both sides perfectly flush. Our kit lockers had to be left open and at all times on view, with our kit all rolled up to the correct size, tied with clothes stops and laid out in the correct order. The pair of boots not being worn had to be on the bottom shelf, soles polished and facing up. These rules also had to be adhered to even when we transferred to the main establishment. Each time we changed kit during the day, it had to be rolled, stopped, and placed in the correct position in the locker. An instructor inspecting the mess at any time would be looking for anything out of place. The following never happened to me, but I've seen it happen to my mates: a particular instructor in the main establishment, who will be featured again later in this story, would empty a locker that he wasn't happy with, walk all over the kit, and leave it to be discovered by the owner on his return. On one occasion, he was waiting at the doorway of our mess when we arrived marching from school. Just inside was a load of kit on the floor; he ordered all of us to walk over it as we entered before removing our boots. We soon learned that it came from three lockers, fortunately not mine—but most of us helped to wash and restore it to respectability.

It has been said that I am what I am because of my training. I would agree that it is partly true, but one thing that I could not tolerate even before *Ganges* was bullying. I must have been about aged twelve at the time when I came across a younger lad whom I knew vaguely from school being tormented by three lads a little older and bigger than myself. I went to his aid, and their leader came at me; I admit that I was terrified at what I was about to receive and must have decided that I had nothing to lose, so I hit him in the stomach and he doubled up and started crying. His mates couldn't believe it; they had never seen their mate cry before and made no attempt to come to his aid. The lad whom I'd helped had run for it. The following day at school, this lad whom I had hit was at the school gate with his mother and he pointed me out as I entered. Next thing I knew, I was sent for by the head and I met again this lad and his mother who had by now told their story. The head asked my side of the story, which I related as above. He then made us lads stand side by side and asked which of us was telling the truth, and then turned to the mother and asked who she thought was telling the truth. She could see that he was much bigger than I was, and she walked across and gave her lad such a smack that he started crying again. I walked out of there feeling about six feet tall, also realising that bullies don't like being stood up to even when their opponent is much smaller.

Back to *Ganges* and the annexe. The one instructor boy was, as you would expect, worse than the other, and if possible I always avoided him. However, our paths did cross regularly, and I couldn't bring myself to respect him and it showed; it seemed that he had his favourites, and I wasn't one of them. A few of us suffered individual punishment from this guy, one such punishment was to have us bend over and be whacked with a hand broom. After suffering this ordeal a couple of times, I threatened to get even. His comment was "You're not big enough," to which I replied, "Even big guys have to sleep." One night I woke in the early hours, collected a broom, and hit him as he lay sleeping; within seconds, the whole mess was awake as he chased me, screaming. Fortunately, the other instructor boy stopped him from killing me after he caught me. I suppose that I should be thankful that I wasn't reported. Within a week, I was receiving another whack from him, and afterwards I said, "Don't forget; you still have to sleep." I don't think he slept well for the next few days in anticipation, but I left it for a week before I hit him again. Much the same happened as the previous time, only this time the other instructor boy threatened us both with Commanders report if either of us misbehaved again.

Shortly afterwards, we left for the main establishment, and within a few days he would have some other poor sods to take it out on.

Whilst still in the annexe, we had our first experience of the much-talked-about, nearly 150 ft tall mast. On our first visit to the main establishment, we were lined up and given a few instructions on what to do and what was expected of us, such as: climb up the ratlines to the first platform, don't go through but climb out round the outer edge and up to the half moon and same again round the outer edge. We would now be about 130 ft high. We were not expected to shin up the remaining more-than-15 ft to the button—that would come later, but climb down on the opposite side.

I remember having to coax, with the help of another boy, a chubby Doug Smith who was terrified. We had only gotten about 15 ft off the ground; he was clinging to the ratlines, but eventually cooperated with us rather than return to the instructor in charge who was giving him a lot of verbal. The other lad stayed alongside him while I followed with my head pushing his ass. Going round the outer edge was the traumatic bit; at one point, he was literally hanging by his arms whilst I was trying to get his feet on a firm footing. He sobbed all the way up and down, and when we did get back on firm ground again, he was still shaking so much that he could barely stand. This took place on the morning of 2 June 1953 on Coronation day, and we were allowed the afternoon off.

Before being transferred to the main establishment, we had to take an exam in order to be allocated in the correct grade—e.g., A/C (advanced course higher or lower), or G/C (general course higher or lower). We also had to stipulate our preference as to whether we wanted to be trained as telegraphists or seamen. At this time, I changed my mind and decided to be a seaman, possibly because telegraphists had to spend eighteen months at *Ganges*, whereas seamen only spent twelve months. Unbeknown to me, my school friend Keith Vale who had joined up with me and had achieved the same speeds in telegraphy as myself decided exactly the same. So we both went over as A/C seamen. Our knowledge of Morse code, semaphore, and signal flags plus seamanship learnt as sea cadets helped us both to cope with the rigours of the remainder of our training. Unfortunately for Keith, he hadn't been as adventurous as I before joining, so climbing the mast and swimming, which he couldn't, put more strain on him than on me.

Two classes shared two instructors, one for seamanship and one for gunnery, we alternated, one week seamanship training and one week gunnery instruction. We also had an officer school teacher who would attempt to further our education, taking up half of our training time each week. Our daily routine was something like: 0600—The duty instructor of the division would wake us, each had his own variation of what we had experienced in the annexe and his own method of punishment for anyone whose feet weren't on the deck when he entered the mess. Once again, it would be a variation of that suffered in the annexe. Much the same routine was followed with regards to making one's bed, dressing, making sure that everything in the kit locker was exactly as it should be, and cleaning and tidying the mess before doubling off to breakfast. Every three days was shower day; we would be awakened earlier and doubled to the shower block with just our towels round us, regardless of the weather. The showers were communal and mostly cold, and before getting dried, we had to go through the humiliation of being inspected by the instructor, who was armed with his torch and lanyard. Every nook and crevice was peered into, and those who weren't circumcised had even that bit inspected, If you didn't feel the sting of his lanyard, you could then dry yourself; if you did, which was usually the case, you had to go through it all again and then double back to the mess.

At 0700, we would double march to the galley for breakfast. We only marched on the parade ground, every other time we doubled. If we were with the gunnery instructor, it would be via the mast. On gunnery week, it would be up and over the mast before and after every meal. On many occasions, he would instruct a number of us to go up to the button and stand and salute before making our way back down again. After breakfast, it was everyone on the parade ground for colours (Raising the flag) and divisions inspection, then off to either school, seamanship or gunnery instructions until lunch time. After lunch, we would change into sports gear; everything taken off was rolled, stopped, and placed in its correct position in the locker. At 1330, we would muster to be detailed for sport, no choice: cricket, football, rugby, swimming, sailing, hockey, and running. What you did depended on where you stood. Afterwards, it was back to the mess, change clothes again, get ready for tea at 1600, and then go to evening instructions until 1830. Then it was dinner and back to the mess if you weren't on duty in the dining hall. If you were, the whole of the dining hall and galley where 2000 boys were fed had to be scrubbed clean. This was done every evening by two classes; our turn came about once a month.

Then we would be back in the mess at about 1930; at 2030 it was cleaning time again and getting ready for nightly rounds, so that hour was really the only free time during the day that we had to write letters or catch up with washing, ironing, etc. At 2045 it was time to turn in, and 2100 was lights out.

The duty instructor would wander around the messes for a while to make sure that we were sleeping and not talking, and on many occasions we were all turned out because someone got caught talking. On a few occasions, our punishment was to go up and over the mast in our pyjamas and bare feet, even with ice on the ratlines.

Saturday morning was work ship. I usually ended up on the pier with many others scrubbing the sailing boats clean with seawater. They were inspected before lunch, and if they passed, you could sail on the afternoon; if they didn't, you scrubbed again instead.

Sunday was divisions; everyone dressed in their best (best uniform, gold badges) and was inspected on the parade ground. This, if I remember correctly, lasted about two hours; after that, I think the rest of the day was our own.

Our seamanship instructor PO was quite a gentleman, and later I believe he went on to become an officer. Although very strict, he was not nearly as sadistic as our gunnery instructor, who was not only a bully but a giant with size twelve boots. He was telling us one day how lucky we were, as in his day they didn't have the luxury of irons. They had to put their kit under the mattress to press it—an idea that one of the lads took up, as the next day was our last before our first home leave after three months. Unfortunately, the GI doing his rounds found the lad's kit under his mattress, as the GI had explained. For this, the whole class was punished; instead of gunnery instructions, we drew rifles and were made to double march up and down the steps known as Faith, Hope, and Charity. Then we had a session on the foreshore where we would do bunny hops—that's hopping along with knees bent and rifle wedged behind the back of the knees—and various other torturous ideas that the sadist could think of.

The following day, we all had to stand naked at the bottom of our beds as the doctor and his entourage came round to inspect us to see if we were fit enough to go on leave the following day. I was amazed that none of them commented on the fact that every one of us had bruising on both shoulders where the 9 lb rifle had been bouncing up and down, as well as behind our knees.

When we returned from leave, we were once again stripped and inspected. I think they were looking mainly for crabs (body lice).

This same instructor made me chew a bar of washing soap for swearing; he was sitting on my bed and I stood in front of him, "Chew but do not swallow, take another bite," he said. I couldn't do so without spitting some out, and most of it went over him. "Don't worry about that, just keep biting, chewing, and spitting till I say stop, then you can wash my clothes." He brought his clothes back for me after he had changed. After that mouth wash, I don't think I tasted my food for the next fortnight. On another occasion, we were on the rifle range and when my target was inspected, it had twenty bullet holes in it instead of ten. Ginger's target, which was next to mine, had none. The GI kicked him and he collapsed. "Crawl down to the sick bay and tell them you fell over a brick," he told Ginger. Unfortunately for him, Ginger told the truth and for once got a sympathetic ear; the GI was removed from *Ganges* as unsuitable. A few years later, I learned that he had died, and I went out with some lads who had also suffered under his reign and celebrated. He was replaced by a completely different personality who was still very strict, but, after his predecessor, was a breath of fresh air. There are many tales of *Ganges*, such as a book written by the late John Douglas. He wrote to ex *Ganges* boys for their input, hoping to write a humorous story—but all he had to work with was tales of hardship and bullying. One comment was, "They had designed the Nazi concentration camps on life at *Ganges*."

HOME LEAVE

It was whilst on one of my leaves from *Ganges* that I met Pat, whom I had known from school. However, it was almost at the end of my leave, and would she be there for my next one?

A couple of days later during this same leave I was walking through the fields in the afternoon with one of my friends who was still at school when we saw a crowd of about six lads and two girls; one of the girls shouted for help, and we walked over to see what was going on, not knowing whether they were fooling around or it was something more serious. Once closer, we could see that both girls were crying. I asked if everything was alright, and the one girl blurted out that the lads were trying to rape them. I suggested that they walk with us, but one of the lads pointed out that there were more of them than of us and started to move in on us. I took my call chain from my pocket (a silver chain that has a bosun's call at the end of it and is worn as part of the uniform in lieu of a lanyard), and lashed out with it. If it hit bare flesh it would draw blood, as it was summer and they were only wearing thin shirts. A scream from the recipient seemed to put the rest off; they followed at a distance for a while, shouting abuse, then eventually found something better to do. We walked and chatted with the two grateful girls, and my friend managed to get a date with one of them. The one I fancied was going away the following day, and my leave would be long finished by the time she got back. Just my luck—two weeks of my leave and I don't meet anyone, then within a few days of the end, I meet two. I was meeting Pat later that evening, and she would still be there on my next leave.

The Mast at HMS Ganges

INDEFATIGABLE

On completion of our training, we travelled by lorry to Ipswich station, then by train via London to Portland to join the Aircraft Carrier HMS *Indefatigable* for our sea training. It would include a short time on the Carrier HMS *Ocean* to prepare her to relieve the *Indefatigable*, which we eventually sailed to Rosythe to be scrapped. We visited Aarhus in Denmark, my first foreign country. On our way, I was manning the helm (steering the ship), probably for the first time, when a message was received that a mine had been sighted in the vicinity. I was quickly relieved by someone more experienced and sent to more menial duties. I never did learn what really happened afterwards, although rumours did filter through that one of the other ships accompanying us did shoot and sink it.

I remember being lined up on the jetty in Aarhus before we were allowed shore leave and told, "Don't forget to behave yourselves, and remember that you're one better than the natives; you're British." The *Indefatigable* still bore some of the scars that she received from a Kamikazi plane that struck her island during WWII. I think if some of the natives had heard those comments, she may have received some more.

After leaving the *Indefatigable* at Rosythe, we were bussed to Edinburgh for another train journey via London to Plymouth.

HMS CARDIGAN BAY

On arrival at Devonport barracks, we were told that we would be flying to the Far East to join the Frigate HMS *Cardigan Bay*. At this time, of course, we had quite a sizeable navy. It was spread out all over the world when most of the map was still red. I know that we still had five battle ships. When I left the navy twelve years later, we had none.

We had two weeks of foreign service leave during which Pat said that she would wait for me. We took the train to London where we were billeted in part of Gooch Street tube station, which had been converted into a transit camp. From there we were bussed to Hendon RAF station where we boarded a converted old York bomber for our flight to Singapore. The journey took a week with three overnight stops; we called at Nice, Rome, Cyprus, Bahrain, Karachi, Delhi, Calcutta, Bangkok, and finally Paya Leba Airport, Malaya. A bus trip then took us to HMS Terror, the naval base in Singapore, where we joined our ship. It was to be our home for the next eighteen months.

When we landed at Cyprus Airport, we noted the wreck of a plane alongside the runway. The pilot had the decency to wait until we were once again airborne before informing us that the wreckage was that of the previous flight on the same mission as ours that had been blown up by terrorists on take-off.

I remember landing in Bahrain and feeling the searing heat as we walked across the tarmac to the airport buildings. We spent an overnight stop in the Great Eastern Hotel in Calcutta, walking the crowded streets of that old city where bodies were lying all over the place, many of which we had to step over. I assumed they were resting and not dead, although many were still there the following morning when we set off for the airport. Our pay at the time was about £2 per week, and I felt highly honoured when I found out the price for staying at that hotel at the time was £17.10s per night. I wasn't very happy about paying 16 shillings for a round of 4 bottles of coke, however.

On our way back to the airport, the bus stopped. I couldn't understand why, as I could see no reason for it until someone said there was a cow lying in the road and that the driver wouldn't allow anyone off to move it. After about ten minutes, it got up and moved of its own accord; it must have been a holy cow.

We soon settled into the ship's routine as we did sea trials, general drills, and exercises to get us into an efficient ship's company.

We'd been out there about six weeks before I got my first mail from home, due to being at sea and the time it took even by airmail in those days. I'd gotten nothing from my family, but a letter from Pat saying how sorry she was to hear of my loss. This confused me somewhat, and I mentioned this to my friend Keith, who had been my school friend and had joined the navy with me. Shortly afterwards he came to me and said, "You'd better read this." It was a letter from his mother saying to pass on his family's condolences on the death of my father. He had been dead for nearly six weeks; apparently, he had died of a heart attack on his way to work a few weeks after his 50th birthday and three months before my 17th. Word soon got to my divisional officer, who sent for me and said that he would get all the details, but that it was no good sending me home, since anything that could have been done would have been done by now. I wasn't given long to grieve; the following day I was manning a rope with others on the capstan. I must have had a blank look on my face, because the same officer shouted to me to stop moping, get a grip, and stop feeling sorry for myself. It seemed a bit harsh at the time, but I suppose he was probably right. If worse came to worst and in a battle men were being injured or killed around me, I would still have to do my job.

A few days later I was given a very boring job by my divisional PO, who told me to take my time over it as he was busy and didn't have the time to sort out a proper job for me. Shortly afterwards, he screamed at me for taking too long, so I answered him back in a way that he didn't take kindly to. He charged me with being insubordinate, to which I said that if he was running me in, I would make it worth his while and took a swing at him. I missed, but as he moved out of the way he cracked his head on a bulkhead strut. On recovering, he took me before the Divisional Officer, who said that he would consider the case. After a while, I was sent for by the DO, who said that due to the circumstances and the heat, and after a discussion with the PO, charges would be dropped. My only regret is I never thanked or apologised to the PO concerned, as if he had pressed charges I could have ended up in prison.

I eventually got the letter from my mother. It had come by sea mail; with all of the upset, she had forgotten to send it by air. In fact, I had other letters from her by air long before this one arrived.

We set off for Hong Kong for a break before going through the Formosa straits up to Korea for the first of many month-long patrols. Eventually we would arrive in Kure, Japan on Christmas Eve. The temperature in Korea was a far cry from the overheated Singapore; we had to chip away the ice from around the anchor before we could drop it. One morning, we awoke freezing as the heating had broken down; we experienced outside temperatures of -30F, which is over 60 degrees of frost in Fahrenheit.

I could never understand what the Koreans were fighting over, as most of what I saw of the place was a barren, hostile land covered in ice and snow during the winter—which for some reason seemed to be most of the time that we spent there. On one occasion, we were anchored off Inchon, and it was arranged that some of the crew would swap places for a couple of days with members of the army based near Seoul, and on their return another group would swap. I was in the first group, and we were taken ashore where we met our counterparts as they disembarked from their lorries. They were all wearing better warm clothing than we were, and most handed over their balaclavas as they said we would be needing them. They were right; it was a bitterly cold place. Our Chief GI was a non drinker, and in the camp canteen that night when everyone was getting merry he asked for a drink of water. He was given a pick and shovel and told to start digging and that if he was lucky, he would find water about ten feet below the ice; he was not amused.

Being involved with the army reminded me of a time as a young boy, shortly after World War II. I was out with a few friends when one of them mentioned that he knew where we could get a rubber dinghy. One of the lads had a baby brother, so we borrowed his pram and walked the mile or so to a compound where the army surplus was stored. Two of the lads went over the fence and a while later returned with a rather large package which they and we struggled with and loaded onto the pram. The compound was just outside the Birmingham boundary, and as we were making our way to the mill pool where we were going to try it out, we spotted a policeman coming over the hill on his bike. Having seen plenty of cowboy films, we knew all about escaping over the border where the sheriff had no jurisdiction, so we ran to cross the border back into Birmingham before he caught up with us. It made not the slightest bit of difference; the Bobby caught up with us and decided to book only the two eldest lads, since they were the ones who had gone over the fence. Someone had spotted them and phoned the police.

It transpired that what we had stolen wasn't a dinghy, but rather a decoy rubber tank, one of the many used to fool the enemy reconnaissance planes into thinking that we were gathering our forces in some place other than the genuine one.

When we returned to the ship, we handed back our balaclavas with grateful thanks and the next group swapped.

On the next groups return, I was detailed as boats crew to ferry the soldiers ashore and our crew from shore to ship.

The boat was bouncing about in the swell alongside the jetty and as I was assisting someone into the boat, the boat lurched and I fell into the icy water, managing to grab the side of the boat so I only went in to the waist. I was quickly hauled inboard and we left for the ship where the ship's doctor gave me the once over, as by this time the lower part of my body had gone numb. I took some thawing out, and my lower body was stiff and ached for some time afterwards—and that was after only a few seconds in the way-below-freezing water.

After each four week patrol, we would return to Japan. Japan was my favourite; our main base was Kure, but we visited many places including the devastation of the two sites of the atomic bombs, Hiroshima and Nagasaki. We also visited Tokyo, Kyoto, Sasebo, Yokahama, Yokosuka, Kobe, Osaka, and the island of Myajima. There was an incident in the Shimonozaki straits in the Inland sea of Japan where we came very close to a collision with a local fishing boat. I did have a few memorable experiences; the following all took place in Kure.

It was quite common for a few of us to go ashore together, then go our own way and arrange to meet up later; some would go shopping, others for tattoos, and some to smoke opium. I'd been to tattooists with them without having a tattoo as well as to opium dens without taking part; hence our arrangements.

I had arranged to meet some friends in a particular bar, and I was the first to get there. It was early evening and still very quiet, and as usual I was greeted by a hostess who would accompany me during my stay, serving my drinks, etc. The bar was divided into small partitioned areas, and I was shown to one of these and joined by my hostess with my drink. Shortly afterwards I was joined by a Japanese man and his hostess, who after a while bought me a drink. When I returned the favour and got my wallet out, he grabbed it—but I was between him and the exit blocking his way. He picked up an empty bottle and seemed only to tap it on the edge of the table and then had this jagged-edged lethal weapon in his hand. I picked up the other bottle and tried to do the same, but couldn't break it. The women had screamed and run off; he lunged at me, and I hit him with my still unbroken bottle, but he had ripped through my jacket and into my arm. Just then two policemen arrived and pinned me to the floor, and it was only the intervention of the two girls that saved me from arrest. The police took away the other guy, and the one girl tended my wound. I still bear the now very faint scars from the skirmish. Shortly afterwards, my friends started to turn up.

On another occasion, I had left my friends to go back to the ship when I heard a girl scream and then sob, and heard what seemed to be a scuffle up an alley that I was passing. It was dark and I went to investigate. It seemed that this drunken Kiwi was trying to rape a young girl whom he had mistaken for a prostitute; fortunately, he could hardly stand and didn't put up much of a fight. I got him on to the main street and left him there. The girl's name was Rituka Abeyama, and she gave me what she called a Sacred Heart (a fob with a picture of the Virgin Mary and baby Jesus) that she had worn as a necklace. It seems that she may have been a Roman Catholic, which was unusual for a Japanese, or so I thought at the time.

My other experience was more pleasant. I was in a restaurant/cafeteria where I had arranged to meet friends, having been shopping, when a girl came up to me. I first thought that she was a hostess or a prostitute. It turned out that she was neither; she had just arrived in Kure and had never seen an Englishman before, although she had learned English. She had recently lost her mother, and her father had been killed during the war. She had inherited some money, had relatives in Kure, and wanted to start a business. I lost interest in what my friends wanted to do after our meeting and met her at every opportunity. Her name was Hisako Nakao, and I called her Suzie. Whilst away, we would write; when we sailed from Kure to another Japanese port, she would meet me there. I visited her relatives with her and was made very welcome. We used to sit on the floor around a low table with a type of quilt over us all, with a charcoal burner under the table to keep us warm whilst we ate. I dread to think now what I was eating, but at the time I did enjoy it, first with a spoon, then with chopsticks. Our relationship lasted for over a year; we talked of marriage, but it wasn't to be. I was very sad to leave Japan for the last time, and on our way south it was announced over the tannoy that Mount Fuji could be seen at over 100 miles away. The belief was that if Fuji could be seen at over 100 miles, you would return. I did see it and I did return a few years later.

One of our POs had spent a lot of the war in a Japanese prison-of-war camp, and when we came alongside the jetty, the dockers tended to be a little indifferent until he started shouting orders to them in their own language. He claimed to not like them, but he did go in search of one of his old prison guards and revisited him more than once. Maybe they weren't all bad.

He was the co-author of the book *90 Years of Navy* in which he told his life story. I believe that he spent over forty years in the service before taking up residence in Kidderminster where he died a few years ago. Another of our crew served on the Destroyer HMS *Kelly* under Earl Mountbatten when he rammed a German warship. Our Captain was also very much decorated for his wartime service, including a DSO and Bar.

We were alongside in Hong Kong at one time when a friend of mine had fallen asleep on a bench seat with folding legs. Unfortunately for him, some movement caused one of the legs to collapse and he slid off and down an open hatch to the deck below. He hit the side of the open hatch to the deck below that, causing himself some serious damage, and ended up in the hospital situated at Hong Kong's peak. He made a full recovery but still bears the scars. I'm still in touch with him as with a few other members of the crew, and through the HMS Cardigan Bay Association, we have a reunion each year.

On one of our many visits to Borneo, we travelled 150 miles inland up the Rejang River. We visited the long houses where the Dyak tribes lived, and met one of their chiefs who wore a necklace of shrunken human skulls around his waist. They were apparently still active in that field around that time. One of our duties whilst in Borneo waters was to protect or go to the assistance of villages attacked by pirates; the most notorious of these went by the name of Mandango Joe. We got the message that he and his associates had rampaged a village not far from where we were and that he had supposedly robbed, raped, and killed there. Shortly afterwards, he was spotted by the lookouts on the bridge and we gave chase, but because of our draft we couldn't get close, as he stayed in the shallow waters. We contacted the inshore police patrols, and they eventually caught him and his gang. I'm not sure how true it was, but we did hear that when he was caught, he was tried, convicted, and executed by sword slashes on the spot. Maybe the police that caught him had lived in that or one of the other villages that had suffered from his evil.

Our travels then took us to Guam in the Mariana Islands. We were the first British warship to visit since World War II and were given a very warm welcome, including a party on the beach. From there, it was another visit to Hong Kong, where some of the crew spent a week on Stonecutters Island practicing for the port rifle competition before another trip through the Formosa straits. We had with us the *St Brides Bay* and the New Zealand frigate *Pukaki*. It was Friday, 13 February 1955 when we were attacked by a MIG 15 who fortunately missed with his bombs. We were then fired upon by the American 7th fleet. They were warning shots, as at that time in those waters we were on opposing sides; the Americans sided with the Nationalist Chang Kai Check of Formosa, and we were there to protect our merchant ships trading with Communist mainland China. We didn't retaliate at the time for fear of creating an international incident. I didn't fancy our chances anyway, considering the might of the 7th fleet and the possibility of a host of MIGs against our three small frigates. It was on our return trip exactly a month later one Friday 13th in March that we had more trouble. We had an SOS from the merchantman Hydroloch, who was being attacked by Nationalist gun boats. We went to her assistance, which resulted in a stand off that lasted most of the night, but no shots were exchanged. When we did get back to Hong Kong, who should also be there but half of the 7th fleet. Whilst ashore, we did have a skirmish, after being confronted by a few crew members of the USS *Bremerton*, the cruiser that apparently fired the shots at us. We were eventually separated by our own and their military police.

It was during a gunnery exercise around this time that I got my timing wrong. I was loading crew on X gun, which is the twin barrelled 4-inch gun at the rear end of the ship. As the gun was facing slightly forward, the procedure was to load the shells, and each loader would go in opposite directions around the gun to collect the next shell, which meant one of us had to pass under the barrels. I should have waited for the gun to fire before passing underneath, but it was pitch black and I was more concerned with doing my job. To my regret, as when the gun went off I was directly below the barrels, and the blast knocked me off my feet and didn't do my ears any good either.

MALAYA

Every six months, we were entitled to seven days of local leave. This was always arranged whilst in Singapore; on one of these occasions, we had the opportunity of spending it with the army, stationed near Kota Tinghi. Who would volunteer to spend a week in the jungle, considering there was a lot of jungle warfare going on with the terrorists during what was known as the Malayan emergency? Some of the crew did. I declined, as I'd heard some of the experiences endured by my brother-in-law who had previously served with the Suffolk Regiment here, and I recall him telling me of one of his experiences. He had gone out on patrol and was ambushed, but the ambush had fortunately gone wrong. It seems that the plan was to let the patrol into a valley, and with a machine gun in front and one behind on high points, they would massacre the patrol. Fortunately, however, the front machine gunner opened fire before the patrol passed the rear gunner; otherwise he would not have lived to tell the tale.

After carrying out exercises off Singapore, we anchored off the Island of Pulau Tioman, just off the coast of Malaya, and were allowed ashore. We didn't see any inhabitants, mainly jungle and a beautiful beach. During our exploring we found bananas growing, so we helped ourselves and took some back for the lads on duty. The duty officer greeted us on our return and asked how much we had paid for the bananas. I, for some unknown reason, said $1.25. Shortly afterwards, those who had brought back bananas were sent for, and we were confronted with the owner of the plantation, to whom we had to apologise. Then we had to pay for and return the uneaten bananas, in addition to receiving a rollicking from the duty officer.

In the eighteen months aboard *Cardigan Bay,* we travelled nearly 100,000 miles at an average speed of 12 knots. We had steamed through many typhoons and hurricanes, visiting Singapore, Hong Kong, Macau, Pulau Tioman, Guam,

Sarawak, Binitang, Sibu, Saraeki, Labuan, in addition to the many places mentioned in Japan, and also Seoul, Inchon, and Pyongyang in Korea.

Most of these places were visited more than once, and some, many times.

After eighteen months, we were all flown home over a two-week period, except a few who chose to return by troop ship. Our return flight only took three days, making an unscheduled stop at Bangkok, then on to Bombay Karachi, Beiroot, Brindissi in Italy, and finally London. I'm not sure, but I think we arrived at Blackbush, as I don't know whether Heathrow and Gatwick existed then. I do remember that it was April and pouring rain. We were bussed to various train stations, depending where we were travelling to. My destination was Euston for the journey to New Street Birmingham and then a taxi home for six weeks leave.

I could now legally go into a pub and drink. I was eighteen and a bit, and I'd been in the Navy for three years.

The Frigate HMS Cardigan Bay

The result of waves breaking over the ship off Korea and freezing.

X Guns Crew in Action.

Transfer at sea to sister ship HMS *St Brides Bay*

SPECIALIST TRAINING

I had written and explained to Pat, my girlfriend, about my liaison with the Japanese girl, but she was still waiting for me. I didn't ask whether she had had other boyfriends. We spent a lot of time together and got quite serious. I suppose I did quite selfishly want someone to come home to on my leaves. I'd gone through the experience of coming home to no one special and then finding someone just before my leave finished, only to find on my next leave that she had found someone else—so sometime in the next six months we got engaged.

At the end of my leave, I reported to HMS *Drake*, the naval base in Devonport where I was told that my application for a Radar course at HMS *Dryad* in Portsmouth had been accepted but wasn't due to start for a few weeks. In the meantime, I was to go on travelling escort duties, meaning that anyone going AWOL and caught by the police would be held at the relevant police station until I and two others arrived to pick them up and return them to barracks where they would be tried and sentenced. Anyone sentenced to Detention Quarters would then be escorted by us to Portsmouth DQ's (Detention Quarters), where they would serve their time. We would then leave on the next train and stop off in Salisbury for a couple of drinks before catching the next train so that we would not return until the early hours of the following morning. This entitled us to an overnight allowance. When a so-called prisoner had finished his time, he had to be escorted back to Devonport, and under these circumstances only one of us would be required. However, I did have one such man ask to be handcuffed to me in case he was tempted to do a runner. I did this job for about a month, doing four or five escorts a week, travelling all over the country by train. It was hardly the worst job I ever had.

I was then drafted to HMS *Dryad* for my Radar course, and it was whilst I was here that I broke my right arm playing football, which made writing rather difficult. As a lot of the course involved chart work and learning to write upside down and back to front, I also had to learn to do it with my left hand. It is something that I wish I had kept up, but now I still strongly favour my right hand.

On completion of my course, I returned to Devonport where awaited me a draft to HMS *Dolphin* to start my training as a submariner. From that day onwards, I was no longer a Devonport rating but a Portsmouth rating, and my official number was changed from prefix D/ to prefix P/.

SUBMARINE TRAINING

I joined Dolphin late in 1956, and also set the date of my wedding to Pat for early April, a couple of weeks before her 19ᵗʰ birthday.

I think I had had an interest in submarines since my school days, as I remember the sinking of the *Truculent* and the *Affray* and reading about the sinking of the *Thetis*. I remember going aboard the *Seraph* whilst at *Ganges*, and whilst on the *Cardigan Bay* made the effort to go aboard the American boat *Sabelo*. It was a boat that I was to re-visit later.

We had so much to learn on this course, but the fascination of it made it fairly easy for me. I particularly enjoyed the week learning how to escape, and as this was the time when the type of escape was in its change. I had to qualify in both, as not all boats were equipped with the latest free assent equipment. We first learnt with the soon to be defunct Davies escape apparatus in a 10 metre deep tank, then into the 100 feet free assent tank.

Apart from the lectures, we also had the simulated experience of escaping from a sunken submarine.

First, we had to experience the decompression chamber, taken to the equivalent depth of 100 feet. Next it was into the tank, where we were taken down in pairs to 5 m in a diving bell where we just breathed from the compressed air trapped in the top of the bell. We wore a life jacket, taking a deep breath and stepping out of the bell, and within seconds we reached the surface.

Our next exercise was to enter one of the side chambers at 30 feet, where probably a dozen of us would crowd in, once again wearing only a swim suit and life jacket. The compartment was then flooded until the pressure was equal to that of the main tank at that depth, so our heads would still be above water and we were able to breathe in the compressed air. The life jacket was fitted with a relief valve to allow the expanding air to escape as we rose to the surface. It also has a toggle on each side for the two instructors waiting outside in the water to grab hold of. The hatch would then be opened, giving access to the main tank. One at a time, we were instructed to duck under the water and out into the main tank, where an instructor would grab hold of the toggles and hold us there until we were breathing out correctly. Once they were happy, we would be set free to ascend to the surface. Instructors would be sited at intervals, and if we stopped breathing out, we would be stopped and held until we continued breathing out.

We did two 30 ft, one 60 ft, and one 100 ft escape. The 100 ft chamber was a simulated submarine compartment complete with escape hatch; in here we would carry out a similar routine, except this time we would each breathe from a mouthpiece on a flexible tube plugged into what was known as the BIBS(built in breathing system).The reason for this is because as the compartment is flooded, the air in that compartment is compressed, and any contamination becomes more concentrated. Or if the boat had been dived for a while, it would contain more nitrogen, which meant that an escapee may die from nitrogen poisoning before he left the boat. To allow for this, submarines carried extra tanks containing the right mixture of 20 percent Oxygen and 80 percent Nitrogen, which fed the pipeline in each escape compartment into which our mouthpieces were plugged. Around the escape hatch was a canvass twill trunk, which was pulled down and secured. Someone would climb the ladder inside the trunk and remove the securing clips that held the hatch shut. The outside pressure would now keep the hatch closed. We would then stand around breathing from the BIBS whilst the compartment was flooded, then once the inside pressure equalled the outside pressure, the hatch would crack open and the twill trunk would fill with water. Once again, to escape we would in turn take a deep breath from our mouthpiece and discard it, then duck under the water into the trunk, and go up the ladder and through the hatch and out into the open sea. In this case, it would be the 100 ft column of water where once again instructors would be waiting for us to make sure that we would make a safe ascent.

When we take in a breath of air, we take in approximately 1 cubic foot at whatever pressure we are surrounded by—e.g., at sea level it would be something like 15 pounds per square inch. At 100 feet depth, the pressure is around 50 pounds per square inch, so that cubic foot that we breathe in at 100 feet is equivalent to roughly 6.5 cubic feet at sea level. Therefore, as we head towards the surface, the excess air in the life jacket escapes through the relief valve, and if we didn't allow the air out of our lungs on our way up, we would probably explode before we reached the surface.

On arrival at the surface, we would leave the water and stand for ten minutes in view of the doctor in case anyone showed signs of the bends. On standby is the recompression chamber. We carried out this escape as we did others, wearing swimsuits and life jackets; in a real escape, we would don Mr Michelin suits as worn by one of our escapees who had to demonstrate the use on the surface. The suit is not to aid the escape, but to protect one against the elements once on the surface. It has its own compressed air bottle that is used to inflate the suit once on the surface; it is also equipped with gloves, a whistle, and light.

Later in my service, we did go to sea with instructions known only to a few to create for exercise a 'Sub Smash.'

Before diving, a signal is sent to HQ giving dive position etc., and time expected to surface,.Once surfaced, a surfaced signal is sent. If that signal is not received by HQ by the stated time, a 'Submiss' alert is broadcast to all concerned, and preparations start being made for search and rescue. If still no signal is received after one hour, a 'Subsmash' is broadcast, and the search and rescue goes into full swing. To help locate the sunken submarine, two marker buoys are carried on board. If possible, these would be released from inside the boat, one situated at each end, attached to a 300 ft length of wire. The buoy, on reaching the surface, would display its light and transmit SOS from its built in transmitter. All of this would happen under ideal conditions, e.g., the boat sinks in less than 300 ft of water and remains upright. However, the possible causes of a boat sinking are many, with as many different possible outcomes. A few possibilities come to light later.

After completing my training I was drafted to HM Submarine *Turpin*.

TURPIN

When I joined *Turpin,* she was just completing a major refit in Portsmouth dockyard. She had been extended by 12 feet to accommodate, among other things, more batteries, making her one of the so-called Super T's. These were capable of 20 plus knots under water, albeit for only 20 minutes—but enough time to be able to take evasive action when needed.

An article in the paper reported that she had cost £420,000 to build during the war, and with this latest refit and previous refits, a total of £1,240,000 had been spent on her. This made her our most expensive and up-to-date submarine. It was £1.66 million for thirteen years of service and much more service to come.

We carried out our sea trials and learned all about the new equipment and about each other as a crew. I then got married, and shortly afterwards brought my wife to live in Portsmouth. This was a complete waste of time because we then started to spend more time in Scottish waters based at Rothesay on the Isle of Bute, and in Irish waters based at Londonderry. When we did get the occasional weekend leave, Portsmouth was just a little too far, whereas Birmingham would have been more easily accessible. We decided that she would be better off in Birmingham for awhile.

As part of our work up, we were running from Inverary on torpedo trials, and each night we had to moor between two buoys. On one occasion, it was a foul night as we came in; it was pouring down rain and the wind was quite strong. The practice was to nose up to one buoy, and one man, the buoy jumper, would jump onto the buoy and have a line thrown to him. He would pass this through the eye and throw it back and get back on board. This line would then be used to pull a larger rope through and secure the boat, but this had to be done at both ends in this case. I was on the after casing and was designated buoy jumper. After the for'd end had a line attached, the skipper then had to manoeuvre the stern close enough for me to jump, bearing in mind that it was pitch black, raining, and blowing a gale, and that communication was by word of mouth only. I managed to land on the buoy, pass the line through, and jump back onto the boat. We already had the line attached to the main securing rope ready to pull it through, but unfortunately the small line surplus was lying on the casing when the skipper had given the order to the Motor room to go ahead to manoeuvre the fore end. Our rope threaded through what is called the bull ring was now running as we put distance from the buoy. Meanwhile, one of the lads had gotten one of his legs tangled in the loose line and was slowly being dragged towards the ring. All of us carried knives and marlin spikes whilst on the casing, but as the weather was so foul, most had theirs on their trouser belt. Since we were wearing oilskins, access to them was very difficult; fortunately, I wore mine on the outside. However, I was also being dragged with the unfortunate Jim, since I had attached myself to him as I tried to cut through the line. I managed to free him with a couple of feet to spare, but unfortunately for Jim, he had lost most of the flesh off the palms of his hands as he had clung to the guard rail and tried to stop himself from going through the ring. He was taken to a hospital and I've never seen him since. We also lost the rope, so we had to carry out the exercise again.

It could be quite pleasant on the bridge in the fresh air at sea in fine weather, although not so nice having to return below to the smell of diesel and unwashed bodies and a variety of other smells that mingled to greet one. When the weather was rough, however, especially on the *Turpin*, as when she was modified I think they used the original gun tower as the conning tower. So instead of the bridge being on top of the fin as most boats were, we were just a few feet above the casing, therefore there didn't have to be much of a swell for us to be completely swamped. In fact this created another problem as the sea was likely to pour down through the conning tower hatch, so the hatch was often shut and we then had to carry out snorting on the surface to allow us to run the engines.

Relieving the OOW and lookout then became a matter of dodging the waves. The relief would enter the tower and shut the lower hatch, and the control room would inform the bridge. When the bridge thought that fit would allow the tower occupant to open the upper hatch, if the timing was wrong—as was more often than not—the relief got soaked, and the tower had to be pumped out before the reverse process could take place to allow the relieved person back into the boat. Normally, the lookouts would relieve each other every half hour, but as it was such an ordeal under these conditions, whoever was first of the watch to go up would usually stay up for the full two or three hours. It was never very pleasant, as whilst standing there wearing a harness clipped to the rail for safety, the sea would not only wash over you but would also surge upwards, filling your sea boots and getting under waterproofs, soaking the rest of your body.

It was now time for us to start doing what we had trained for, which was to go on what were commonly known as mystery trips. Leaving harbour at night, we would paint out our identifying number, dive shortly afterwards, and make our way to much colder climates, i.e., the Arctic. We would not surface again until we were back just outside our port of departure, anything between eight and twelve weeks later. We were not allowed to transmit by Radio or use Radar. For this reason, the Radar equipment was removed to make space for more listening gear, SHFDF (Super High Frequency Direction Finder), commonly known as shuff duff. So we could receive radio messages but not transmit, and we could listen to other Radar but had none to use ourselves. This way we could not give away our presence to any eavesdroppers. SONAR would not transmit, but we rarely did anyway; we would do as normal and listen. Other precautions were to batten the escape hatches from the outside, so that in the event of being depth charged they would not spring open. As we couldn't use the escape hatches, the escape equipment was redundant, so all of that would be left behind, leaving more storage for creature comforts. The marker buoys were also left behind.

From what I understood, there were two reasons for these excursions: (1) To be strategically placed if war should break out, which is why we carried a full complement of torpedoes. (2) To carry out photographic surveillance of their warships through the periscope, listen to radio messages ,and identify new radars and radar installation sites. We would also carry a few extra bodies, secret types, some linguists, and some maybe to listen to what we might say after being on watch, as we were advised to not speak of our experiences amongst ourselves or to anyone else at a later date. I hope I am now free to do so after I believe thirty years have passed, and I dearly hope that I am not restricted by the seventy-five year rule as far as official secrets are concerned. I did speak to someone recently, not a submariner, but one of the secret types whom we took along with us. He had been in touch with someone at the ministry of defence regarding a campaign to get some sort of award or recognition for those of us who undertook these operations, and was told categorically, "It never happened."

It would take about two weeks to reach our patrol area, during which time we had to avoid being detected by our own defences. So we would travel by battery power during the day, and snort to recharge the batteries at night.

TECHNICAL:

The submarine has two diesel engines, and the Super T has four main Electric Motors as opposed to two on other boats. The combination is: diesel engine, clutch, motor, clutch, motor, clutch, drive shaft, screw, on either side. This combination makes it very versatile considering that the motors can also be used as generators. On the surface, on passage the boat may be driven in direct drive, i.e., all clutches engaged so that in effect the engine is driving the boat. At the same time, the motors are also being turned so that if needed they can also generate power to charge the batteries. Normally the engine would be used to drive the forward motor by engaging the first clutch, and this motor is used to generate power to recharge the batteries. The second clutch is disengaged. The rear motor is then used to drive the screw under battery power via the engaged third clutch and prop shaft; this is also the usual method whilst snorting.

SNORTING:

An engine needs air to run, so whilst submerged to run the engines, we have to take in air. To do this, we use a method basically the same as the one that a swimmer uses when snorkelling (snorting). We have a snort mast, which we raise the same as we raise a periscope. Its principal is more like the old type of snorkels with the ping pong ball fitted to stop the intake of water. In rough weather, this can be a painful operation, as each time mast dips below the surface the valve is closed and the engines continue trying to suck in air, creating a vacuum in the boat. Then the mast clears and the valve reopens, letting in the air, and normal pressure is resumed until the next dip. You may have had a similar experience when flying, when the pressure affects your ears. Imagine what it's like occurring sometimes every minute for eight or more hours a day for ten weeks.

The chef used to love these conditions, especially when baking bread. If the boat was in a state of vacuum at the critical time, the bread would turn out big and fluffy. However, if the pressure came back at the wrong time, we'd end up with something good enough to build a house with. Also, of course, in this part of the world the air that is being sucked in is something below zero, making life even more uncomfortable. If the mast does not clear the surface after a time, not enough air is available and the engine stops. It probably takes fifteen minutes to shut off and restart snorting again.

Whilst dived and under battery power, one disengages the clutch between the engine and the forward motor and if the clutch between the motors are engaged so that there are two motors in tandem. Running them in this set up at full speed gives you twenty knots plus, which is ideal for manoeuvrability if a destroyer is homing in on you with a load of depth charges.

Once in our patrol area, we would remain as quiet as possible, i.e., use only one motor at slowest speed during surveillance periods, travelling at about 1.5 knots. This also helped conserve battery power; very little cooking took place for the same reason.

Battery conservation was always a major priority, as we could never be sure that it would be safe to recharge when we needed to do so, or for how long it would be safe.

After a few days at sea, any fresh food would have been long gone; our daily diet was weetabix and tinned milk for breakfast, salad (i.e. cold tinned peas), carrots, and a variation of cold tinned meats or tinned herrings and POM (a form of modern day Smash for lunch)—and something similar for dinner. Occasionally whilst snorting, if the skipper thought things were quiet and safe, we did get a cooked dinner. If conditions allowed, we did have bacon and egg on Sundays for breakfast. That was the only way we got to know what day it was, until the eggs ran out or went rotten. Then it was bacon and tinned tomatoes. The fresh bread that we took with us didn't last long; after a few days, it would start to go mouldy. We would cut off the mould and still eat what was left until we got down to an edible piece the size of an Oxo cube. That's when the chef would gamble with the elements and bake bread, if conditions allowed whilst snorting.

Another hardship that we experienced was the lack of fresh water. We had fresh water tanks that were filled before we left, and we also had distillers, but the use of these was avoided as much as possible as it occupied another man. It also used precious amps and would only provide about 1.5 gallons per hour of fresh (if you could call it that) water. It was only used for drinking or cooking; washing in it was certainly discouraged, and we never had the luxury of showers anyway. There was plenty of sea water of course, cold only—and have you ever tried getting a lather. Once a week, I took to having a wash down in white spirits, being careful where it was applied of course.

Nuclear submarines don't have this problem, as they end up with a surplus of fresh water through their reactor cooling system.

We had plenty of hair raising moments on these trips, as we did on many of the more mundane operations. During darkness at periscope depth, the boat was darkened down to minimum lighting throughout, and the control room was completely blacked out so that the officer of the watch looking through the periscope did not have his vision impaired while peering into the black night. We carried out our duties by luminous dials and minimum red light indicators. Also under these conditions, we had two officers of the watch, one on the periscope and one keeping the trim by moving ballast water about or even pumping water out or taking water on to keep the boat on an even keel and at the right buoyancy. At one such time, we were snorting and I was on the fore planes keeping depth when I noticed that just as it had been a few hours earlier when I had been on watch, I was having difficulty keeping the boat down. In other words, the fore end was light. I mentioned this to the OOW. who replied that he couldn't pump any more water forward as there was no more capacity. I suggested that maybe we had an air leak into number one main ballast. Ballast tanks are situated outside the pressure hull and are flooded to submerge and blown to surface; the top is fitted with a hydraulically controlled vent, and the bottom has a free flood hole. On the surface, the tank is full of air, with the vent shut keeping the boat afloat. To dive, the vent is opened, allowing the air out and the water in through the hole in the bottom; once submerged, the vent is closed, ready at any time for the HP air to be blown in, pushing the water out through the bottom hole. This would bring the boat back to the surface. The OOW then asked the man on the dive panel to check for a leak. As you may know, HP air through a pipe makes it very cold. This is what he was checking, and the answer was no. I then asked about if it was only a minor leak, as it had been like this for a long time and could have emptied the tank over a long period. "I'll prove it to you Harris," he said, and then did something that nearly finished us. "Open one main vent," he ordered. Within seconds, the boat had taken on about ten tons of water at the fore end, and we went down like a brick at a very steep angle. I changed my planes from full dive to full rise instinctively, but it didn't help much. Just then the Captain appeared and gave the order "Blow one main ballast." Fortunately, the guy on the panel had had the sense to close the vent. Unfortunately, at the same time that the OOW had given the order "Full astern," the bow had come up and we were hurtling down stern first. There are two depth gauges fitted by which to keep depth; one operates to a depth of 150 ft, and the other down to 600 ft. Below 150 ft, the shallow water gauge is shut off, which I did as we plunged below. When the boat was built some fifteen years earlier, she was deemed safe at 500 ft, but over the years and some surgery to the hull, the safe depth had been reduced. Our safe depth at that time would have been about 300 ft. I do know for certain that we went below 600 ft, because the needle was on the stops at that depth, and it was quite awhile after we got the boat under control before the needle moved off its stop. Our sudden plunge also created another problem: as a boat goes deeper, it also gets smaller and heavier, and the OOW would normally pump water out to compensate and take water on as we rose. If we hadn't gotten control in time, we would have plummeted farther and faster until we crushed under the pressure. We were very lucky to survive, especially having gone so deep. What the OOW should have ordered was "Open and shut one main vent," thereby restricting the amount of water taken in.

I didn't think that my perseverance in solving the problem was going to nearly kill us all. But then we might have ended up even deeper if we had unintentionally surfaced and been spotted by an aircraft or ship and been attacked. I was never privy to what the Captain said to that particular OOW afterwards, but I don't recall ever seeing him again after we eventually returned to Gosport.

The first thing to do on arrival at Dolphin, of course, was to have a bath before going home, to try to get rid of the smell of diesel and the bodily smells that that, having lived with for so long, one got used to. However, even after a bath, I noticed that people chose to not sit next to me on the bus, and when I got home, my wife suggested that I have a bath with plenty of added fragrance.

We did a couple of these trips before we headed off in the opposite direction with the home fleet to the West Indies on exercises. I think the trip to Jamaica should have taken about two weeks, but after about a week at sea both of our engines broke down, so we were unable to make way with them, and the batteries couldn't be recharged. Thank God this didn't happen whilst we were on a mystery trip. The Flag officer told us to make our way as best we could. We did this by running one motor slowly to preserve battery power; what should have taken us another week took us another three. Once in warmer climes the skipper would stop the boat and let us have a swim every few days, with instructions to stay close to the boat. I remember getting back on board with one of the other lads who had also been chasing after a makeshift ball and had gone further out than the Jimmy liked. He called us both to him and told us that we were banned from the next two swimming sessions by way of punishment. I looked past him and pointed, "Don't worry sir, I won't be going again," as a huge dorsal fin was passing a few feet away.

We eventually arrived in Kingston, Jamaica and berthed alongside our depot ship HMS *Maidstone*, which had arrived two weeks ahead of us. We would now have an inboard mess and bathroom facilities; she also carried most of our kit, as being short of space on the boat, anything not required during the voyage would be left inboard.

The engines were worked on with spares and help from the *Maidstone,* and a few days later we were declared fit to continue with fleet exercises and make our way to Barbados. Shortly after leaving harbour, we broke down again, and we had to limp back into Kingston. However, there was now no berth for us, as merchant ships had taken those occupied by the Royal Navy, so we had to request a berth alongside a merchantman, until such a time as she put to sea when we would have to beg again. This went on for about two months; it was the best and most restful time that I had during my twelve years. During our stay, we were accommodated in the army barracks of the Royal Worcestershire Regiment. Kit wise, we only had what we stood in, as the rest was on the *Maidstone.* In order for us to go ashore looking respectable, it was decided that the army would supply us with a pair of army KD trousers and that we would have to buy our own shirts. "But," said the Jimmy, "We must wear our caps." Our shirts were quite something for that era—bright yellows, reds, greens with various slogans such as, "Take her to Jamaica where the rum comes from" splashed over them. I remember a few of us walking down a street and being met by the Provost Marshall who gave us the third degree about our dress. We were told to return to barracks and await the outcome. Apparently the PM's comment to the Jimmy was, "If we are going to send our sailors ashore dressed like pirates, could we not advertise the fact that they are members of the Royal Navy and discard the hats?"

We spent mornings working, cleaning, and maintaining the boat, and if we weren't on duty watch when we had to stay on the boat, we had the rest of the day to ourselves. Afternoons would be spent in the barracks pool or maybe on a trip into town for a drink and a swim in one of the many lovely hotels. The name of one I recall was the Myrtle Bank. I also remember being confronted by about a dozen Jamaican lads, who were asking questions like, "Is it true that we can come to your country and not work and still get paid?" Word was getting back. They turned out to be a good crowd and offered to supply some entertainment, as they were members of an all-steel band. They arranged a venue; all we had to do was get the rest of the crew there. Everyone had a good night.

Like all good things, it had to come to an end, and a tow was arranged to take the boat to Plymouth for engine repairs. As the whole crew would not be required for this exercise, most of us were distributed amongst the fleet to take passage back home, and a few ships were diverted to pick us up. I took passage on the destroyer HMS *Camperdown.* Our first port of call on route was the lovely Jamaican resort of Montego Bay, where we stayed for a few glorious days. On one of those days, four of us were having a quiet drink early evening when this Liverpudlian introduced himself to us and invited us to his club later that evening. He did say that we wouldn't be able to afford the drinks, as the cheapest drink, a glass of water, cost fifteen shillings—but said that we should ask for his partner who would supply us with our first round, and that thereafter since we were in uniform, more drinks would be offered by the visiting stars than we would be able to consume. It was a night to remember.

We next called at Hamilton, Bermuda where we hired mopeds and explored the island, a fascinating place. We must have travelled around it a few times, as our mopeds were good for 200mpg and the island isn't very big, but with a full tank of one gallon, we managed to run out of petrol.

Our next port of call was Halifax, Nova Scotia. My only recollection here was meeting a Canadian couple who said they knew a good place to eat and drove us a hundred miles and back again and thought nothing of it. I think Alan Ladd and another star were on the next table. I do remember that she was taller than he was; in fact, he was quite short. From there, it was across the Atlantic and home for the middle of April. I think my son was conceived shortly afterwards, as he was born the following January. He was a strapping 9 lb 2 oz baby, unlike my daughter, eighteen months later, at 4 lb. She was conceived after one of the following mystery trips that we resumed once the boat was declared fit again.

Whilst the boat was being fixed, I was allowed to spend time on a course for promotion to Leading Seaman. I was also detailed for a course as Navigators Yeoman, and finally the whole of the attack team, of which I was a member, went off for two weeks to Rothesay on the Isle of Bute to brush up our skills in the attack teacher. After two weeks of writing backwards and upside down, my letters that I attempted to write the normal way were difficult for my wife to decipher.

I remember returning to the boat to help put the final touches and painting her to get her ready for sea. Many of us favoured Naptha to white spirits for cleaning paint brushes, and we needed some. I presented the Jimmy with an order for him to authorise of 10 gallons of Naptha. He looked down his nose at me and said, "Why do you have to abbreviate everything?" and changed the order to read 10 gallons Napthalene, which I took to the dockyard stores and presented to the store man. "Sorry," he said, "We only supply naphthalene by weight." "Okay," I said, "I'll take the equivalent in weight." "What transport do you have?" "The small van outside," I replied. "You'll never get it all in there; you'll need a box lorry." "What, for two drums of naphtha?" "No, for 160 lbs of mothballs." I had to return and relay my tale to a red-faced Jimmy, who didn't think it funny as he rewrote the order for Naphtha.

Once ready again for sea, we left for Scottish waters to put the boat and crew through their paces to make us ready for further mystery trips. Whilst running from Loch fine, we had a flu epidemic on board. Half of the crew were laid up ashore in Nissan huts whilst the other half went out in the early hours each day carrying out various sea trials and returning late evening to tend those who were sick. Most of the crew were ill, but to qualify as sick one's temperature had to be over 101 F, so the sick list varied from day to day.

One cold, wet, miserable Sunday whilst in Arrochar after tot time, someone had the bright idea that we should climb Ben Cobbler. A dozen or so donned their foul weather clothing and, as I had work to do first, I said I would set out a few minutes later and catch them up. The only sea boots (Wellingtons) that I could find were both left footed, but spurred on by my and half of someone else's rum ration, I set out to catch up. After about half an hour, I caught sight of them, and they stopped and waited for me. Once I caught up, I asked if anyone had two right footed sea boots, but no one did, and they set off again with me struggling to keep up. We managed to get quite a ways up but never managed the summit; I don't think we were really equipped for it.

We had arrived back to Arrochar late one night and set off for the only pub, the Arrochar Hotel. There was some altercation with the manager and a guy we called Big John; afterwards, John said, "If he speaks to me like that again I'll have him." Unbeknown to us, the manager had called the police. When they arrived a while later and asked what the problem was, the manager said "That big guy said he's gonna have me." The policeman said "Okay, Sir, when he's had you, we'll have him."

We then carried out some fleet exercises around the Northern tip of Scotland; another of our submarines was also taking part. We were at periscope depth snorting, and I was on watch manning the shuff duff and listening for other Radars when I heard a very strong Racket (Radar transmission) extremely close, which I recognised as a submarine radar. Rather than go through the usual procedure, I opened the radar office door and shouted into the control room, "Submarine racket dangerously close, suggest we go down PDQ." I didn't get a reply, but the order was given "Flood Q 200 feet." The reason for my concern was that if we didn't know she was so close, she probably didn't know we were there either, and a collision would probably have been fatal for over 130 men. The OOW obviously thought the same, and didn't question my actions. Once down without the noise of the engines running, the SONAR reported Submarine HE bearing 080. A few seconds later, we didn't need sonar to tell us that she was passing overhead.

Speaking of opening the radar office door reminds me that around that same time whilst doing much the same, I heard over the tannoy: "Radar operator to the control room." The boat had been taken deep, so shuff duff was ineffectual. Unfortunately, there was a sliding door on the radar office and, as explained earlier, as the boat goes deeper it also gets smaller. Under these conditions, it's impossible to open the radar office door, so I was trapped. I explained my predicament over the tannoy. "Give it ten minutes," came back the reply from the Captain, "We'll go back up to periscope depth when I think it's safe."

By this time, we were ready for our next mystery trip, so it was back to the depot Ship HMS *Adamant* at Faslane in Gareloch to store ship and make ready for our coming ordeal.

The day before we left was a Sunday, and at that time, to qualify for a drink in Scotland on a Sunday you had to be a traveller; to qualify as a traveller, you had to have travelled three miles. The nearest small town of Helensburgh was just over three miles away where we would drink in the hotel there. We would stay there for a couple of hours before catching the train into Glasgow, where we would go to the dance at the NAAFI club. The train was the compartment type with no corridor or access to toilets. In the crowded compartment with us were two attractive young girls who were very quiet, and no one offered to speak to them. One got out at one of the stops but jumped back on as soon as the train set off again, and did the same again at the next stop. It seemed as though she was trying to get to a toilet, but the train didn't stop long enough. After this, as the train was well under way, she said, "If I don't have a pee, I'm going to wet myself," and promptly opened the window, dropped her pants, and said, "Help me sit on the window so I can pee outside." A couple of the lads obliged as the rest of us looked on in amazement.

I think it was a couple of trips later, or maybe even my last on the *Turpin* that we had another frightening time. We found ourselves in the middle of the Russian fleet who were carrying out exercises with their latest submarine, which was probably why we were sent there. We could hear them pinging, trying to locate her, when we picked up her HE (hydrophone effect). I was at my attack station behind the plot. Sonar listen for HE (other ships propeller and engine noises) and can distinguish to a degree what type of ship, or at least what type of engine (i.e., Diesel or Reciprocating, Submarine or torpedo etc.) it is. This information they pass to the control room for everyone to hear; they also pass the info to me continuously along with the bearing and give it a reference. With the attack team closed up, we would have two sonar operators, one sweeping either side relaying the info, and I would plot the info of all of the ships onto the plot. I did so by drawing a graph showing their movements and speed and writing backwards on a Perspex plot so that the Captain the other side of the plot could read it a glance. At this time, I had the submarine, two destroyers, and a few others, which we were not too concerned with unless they came closer. They were searching in another direction. We could hear the pinging from the two destroyers searching for their sub when they located us. We assumed that they thought that we were theirs; we were trying to keep a parallel course with their sub, and each time she turned, we had to follow. We didn't know how deep she was and we didn't want her to detect us, but our boats were renown to be quieter than theirs, and staying slightly behind her lessened her chances of detecting us because of her own screw noise. We played like this for what seemed to be hours. I remember reaching the top of the plot and restarting at the bottom a few times. Nerves were a bit tense, and then we heard a series of grenades exploding. When exercising between ship and submarine, communication is not easy, as you can imagine. Rather than search all day in the wrong direction and waste a lot of exercise time, a ship will use a series of grenades to ask questions or give instructions (i.e., 'Indicate your position,' 'Surface,' etc.). We would obviously know the code that our ships use, but we did not know what the Russian code was, so their explosions meant nothing to us. All we could do was take evasive action and try to get out of range of their sonar. We went deep, speeded up, and carried out various other manoeuvres. Eventually they lost contact, and we laid low for a while. We can only assume that whatever number of grenades they dropped must have been the request to indicate our position; in our case, on exercise we would have fired a smoke candle. I'm not sure what their procedure would have been, but the surface ships must have realised from their indication that what they had been shadowing was not the same boat, and suddenly every ship above seemed to be pinging in our area. They managed a couple of hits, then lost us again. They decided to let us know that they were on to us and dropped depth charges, a frightening experience—although not close enough to do much damage. It made me wonder about how some of my predecessors during the war must have suffered. The only damage that I can recall was that we were unable to use one of the four toilets, and when we eventually surfaced off the Isle of Wight, part of the casing was missing. On a couple of other trips of this nature, when we thought we were in danger of detection we headed for the ice for shelter, but on this occasion I think we were too far away.

On returning to Gosport just before Christmas, I once again reported to the sick bay regarding a throat infection, which I had been suffering with on and off for some time. Each time, it was suggested by the doctor that I go to the hospital to have my tonsils removed, but the Jimmy had overridden this as I was needed on the boat. However, he would release me next time in port, until the next time came. On this occasion, the doctor got a higher authority to demand that I be released for serious health risk reasons, and an appointment would be made for me in early January.

I was duty on Christmas day, and we were berthed alongside what was known as Petrol Pier with the Aeneas outboard of us. Both boats were lit up with light decorations, since it was Christmas, and there was something of a party going on aboard the *Aeneas*. I had a three-hour stint as trot sentry during the late afternoon/ early evening, being responsible for the boat's safety and security. It was during this time that a number of the party goers decided to leave the *Aeneas*, crossing my boat and down the gangway onto a pontoon before going up a ladder onto the pier. As one of the merrymakers walked down our gangway, he fell sideways and took the gangway sideways with him, and he fell in the water between the pontoon and the boat and didn't surface. It seemed to me that he had gone down and come up under the pontoon. It was a cold, wet, miserable day, and I was dressed accordingly; nevertheless, I lay on the pontoon head and shoulders under the water feeling around for him. The cold water had sobered him up enough to want to live, as he was trying to find a way out, and I managed to help him out. By this time he had taken in a fair bit of water, and a couple of his mates helped him down to the sick bay where he made a full recovery. His name was Whimpy Baldwin, and I met him again a few years later. Meanwhile his little escapade had put out all of our decorative lights, which had not gone unnoticed by our duty officer, the First Lieutenant, who turned up to investigate. On hearing my story, which was supported by a witness, he commended me. Later when he returned and found me missing from the casing for a few minutes more than was allocated to carry out my rounds, he wanted to charge me with being absent from place of duty until I pointed out that we were charging batteries and that I was also responsible for switching on the Hydrogen eliminators, which adds time to the other responsibilities.

Shortly afterwards, I was drafted to RNH *Haslar,* and my tonsils were removed. I learned later that my wife and son came to visit, who were now living in Gosport. A few others had also had the same operation on the same day, and she was directed to the guy in the next bed to me. They told her, "He's okay, unlike him in the next bed," pointing to me. "We thought we had lost him, but managed to resuscitate him." She took one look and nearly dropped our son. I think we were kept in for about a week, and then we had to see the senior medical officer who would decide what happened next. I was expecting at least a week of sick leave, but got, 'Back to duty.' All of the others who had the same operation got two weeks of sick leave. I queried this, first with the Sister who took me to the surgeon, and then back to the SMO who informed me that it was requested by my First Lieutenant that I be returned to my ship ASAP. I explained that we were going to sea. "Ah!" he said, "The fresh air will do you good." "I'm a submariner," I replied, "and we will be under water for about ten weeks." He was none too pleased, and instructed my doctor to arrange for me to have two weeks sick leave. Then he spoke to my First Lieutenant, a conversation to which I was not privy.

TRESPASSER

On returning from sick leave, I reported to *Spare Crew*, as the *Turpin* was now two weeks into another mystery trip. On my first day, I was sent to the dockyard with someone to retrieve a gangplank. As we could barely lift it once we located it, I rang the office for more help. I was told, "Leave it and get back here; you're joining the *Trespasser* which is sailing this afternoon."

I reported to *Trespasser* and asked how long we would be away, so that I could let my wife know. "Oh you'll be back by the weekend." The trouble was that he didn't say which weekend; it was six weeks later when we arrived back in Gosport. The *Trespasser* was one of the few boats that still had an open bridge and four-inch gun mounted and a gun tower in addition to the conning tower. We had spent most of the time running around the Scillies carrying out target practice. As I had been drafted as a gun layer and not as an RP, part of my remit was guns crew. The Captain of the gun, who was actually the resident gun layer, gave us all instructions as to what was expected of each of us. I was detailed as the trainer. The layer's job is to site the gun vertically and fire it; this takes experience since, as you can imagine, the boat is never still. My job as the trainer was to site it horizontally, which is not quite so difficult if you know what the target is among the many in those waters. The routine is for the boat to come up to periscope depth, and the Captain will identify the target and show the guns Captain. Air is released into the boat to create a pressure, and the gun layer goes up the tower first, empty handed, and will open the hatch when ordered, usually when the hatch is about six feet below the surface. The extra pressure in the boat aids this, and he goes out with the air bubble, opens the breech of the gun, and prepares for firing. The second man out is the trainer, carrying a shell, who doesn't have the aid of the air bubble but catches all of the incoming water, as does anyone else in the tower. Once out, he loads his shell and takes his place on the training controls. He is then followed by the loader, also with a shell; the rest of the guns crew form a chain to supply the loader. As the trainer, I try to find the target, although I haven't a clue what it looks like and there are plenty to choose from. The layer knows, as he was shown it, but can only move the barrel up and down; eventually, with his guidance I find it, and we fire a few shots, secure the gun, get below, and go through it all again. Before our next run, the Captain who timed us said that we needed to do it faster. I suggested to the Captain that I thought it wise that the target be pointed out to me also, as it would save time if I knew where it was and what to look for. He didn't agree; I don't think he was conversant with our differing roles until after about four attempts. Then he followed us onto the bridge and saw for himself my point, and I was allowed a sighting through the periscope before going up the tower on future shoots.

We did a lot of this, and as we got better, we also did night shoots. All of this was interspersed with exercises with ships from Plymouth and Portland; we would hide, and they would try to find us. We did spend the odd day in Falmouth, and on one occasion a friend of mine, Tony, who liked his drink, went ashore. I was surprised to find him back early and sober. Apparently, he claimed to have seen the light, having talked with a member of the Salvation Army. He had stopped drinking, turned to the church, and eventually married a girl from the church. Tony will be mentioned again later in the story.

We arrived in Gosport on the Friday and I was drafted back to spare crew. On Monday, I was invited to visit old friends on the *Turpin* at tot time, an hour or so before she sailed. It was fatal; the Jimmy spotted me and said, "You'll be sailing with us then Harris." I thought he was joking, so I replied, "I'll just nip home for my tooth brush then." "You know enough of the crew; borrow one. I'm serious, you're coming with us." Fortunately, it was only for just over a week.

AENEAS

On returning to Gosport, I was looking forward to spending some time with my family. On arrival, I learnt that the *Aeneas* was going to sea the following day, and as they were short of an RP, I would be going with her. So I spent one night at home before taking to the depths once more.

Like the *Trespasser*, *Aeneas* still had all of her wartime features—the gun, open bridge, external tubes, etc. The main difference, of course, is that one was T class and the other was A class.

The T class was the earlier model, with rounded ballast tanks, and when the toilet is used, it has to be individually discharged. The A class had almost square tanks, and toilets discharge into a main tank, which is discharged when safe and convenient.

I spent about three months on the *Aeneas* but I don't recall much of my time on board except the last day:

We arrived in Gosport on a Friday after being at sea for a while. On Saturday morning, I was told that I was leaving the boat, as I was required in spare crew. I reported to the office, who drafted me back to the *Turpin*. I went aboard and met some of my old friends, including the Jimmy. Apparently, the guy who had relieved me when I went into the hospital had fallen foul of the Jimmy. When at the helm, there are also other duties to carry out, one of them being control of O port main line suction valve which is sited alongside the helmsman next to Q main line suction. O port is used regularly whilst dived on instructions from the OOW to move water as ballast for the trim, and is easily opened and also smooth to the touch. The Q valve is knurled and needs a wheel spanner to open it. O tank is a trim tank. Q tank is the tank that is flooded to make the boat ten tons heavier when you need to dive quickly (i.e., if at periscope depth and a ship or an aircraft is sited, the order would be given, "Flood Q 100 Feet," and the guy on the dive panel would open Q vent and once at a safe depth would give the order: "Shut Q, Blow Q." Then "Vent Q inboard.")

The valve that my relief opened is only used if Q tank for some reason needs to be pumped out. I'm not sure how he managed to open it, but it could have caused a tragedy if it had not been noticed, and it got him thrown out of Submarines. Apparently, they had been at a hundred feet and miles from land, and Jimmy had been screaming at him to get off his boat "NOW."

Jimmy had gone into the spare crew office on return to Dolphin looking for a replacement and spotted my name. He wanted me so he got me—not for long though, as the *Trump* was also short of an RP and was going to sea that afternoon. I was drafted back into spare crew once again and was told to wait outside Commander S/M's office whilst the two Jimmys fought over who would get my services. *Trump* won, so I sailed with her that afternoon. I believe that I hold the record for being the only man to have served on three submarines and two spare crews on one Saturday morning.

TRUMP

By this time, my wife had gotten used to me taking what were known as pier head jumps, which was just as well because there were more to come. So, having spent one night at home, I was back to sea on yet another boat, and on one occasion we were exercising off the Channel Islands when tragedy struck.

We were at periscope depth at night, so as explained earlier, the control room was in complete darkness. The OOW was on the periscope, and occasionally, as was normal, he would give the order to lower periscope to clear the lens. If work is to be carried out on the scope, or if a man for some reason has to go into the periscope well, the scope would be fully raised and the lugs on the scope would be lined up with those on the deck head. Also, pins would be fitted to take the weight of the scope in case the hydraulics should fail. Unfortunately, the OOW was holding onto the deck head lugs when he gave the order to raise periscope, and he lost two fingers off one hand and damaged his other. Whilst waiting for the helicopter to arrive, I was asked to go down the well to find his fingers in case they could be somehow re-attached. I spent a few seconds fishing around in the oily sludge and brought them up; they had been sliced cleanly off. I gave them to the Captain and they went off to the hospital with the patient, but we heard later that unfortunately nothing could be done with them.

The Jimmy was supposedly related to royalty. He also liked to cook, and as he was the duty officer, he cooked a fancy meal for the duty watch of which I was part. The following morning, I bumped into him in the galley frying bacon and eggs for his breakfast. He asked me if I enjoyed the meal, and we started chatting. I can't remember where the conversation went, but he then said, "You think I'm a bastard don't you?" As it all seemed very friendly, I replied, "Yes, but I've known worse." "Do you realize who you are talking to? I'm 85th in line for the throne." "Oh," I said, "You're not an ordinary bastard then, you're a royal bastard," and made a hasty retreat, to be followed by a few pots and pans and anything else he could find to throw.

This was around the time when princess Margaret was about to get married, and Jimmy got his invitation. The skipper, a Southern Irishman, asked the Jimmy if he could get him an invite. He obviously couldn't, so the skipper said, "In that case you will be required on board for duty that day."

I can't remember where we were, but most of the crew had gone ashore and some of the officers arrived back on the boat with guests. The Jimmy (who loved his cocktail parties) asked me if I would help the steward with one such event. Knowing that there would be a few drinks in it for me, I agreed.

After this, I was asked on many occasions to help with arranged parties, and sometimes to organise some impromptu ones in the absence of the steward. Once whilst we were in Gosport where I lived with my wife, I was on board in married quarters as part of the duty watch when I was again asked if I would help, serving drinks and helping myself to the occasional 'Horses neck' (Brandy and dry ginger) as was agreed. When I looked around, it seemed that everyone was pissed except me. I think I must have already had too much, as I took the half empty bottle of brandy that I was using to top up the guests' glasses and topped it up with dry ginger and proceeded to drink it. The First Lieutenant asked me for a drink, so I poured it from the bottle that I was drinking from, missed his glass, and fell over in front of him. He was not too pleased, as he made quite clear, and he told me to get off his boat and not come back until I was sober. I somehow found my way home with the help of a taxi. The following day, I didn't turn up until nearly lunchtime, just about sober. Jimmy caught me, wanting to know where the hell I had been. He reiterated his disgust for letting him down and told me that I had been absent without leave and would be punished. I reminded him that the last thing I remembered him saying to me was, "Don't come back until you are sober." "Well, I think I am now."

On another occasion we were in Copenhagen; once again, I was part of the duty watch, and the Navigating officer was the duty officer, when guests from the British Embassy arrived with the Captain and other officers who had been visiting the embassy. The duty officer requested my services. As you can imagine, Submarines are somewhat short of space, so every nook and cranny is put to use. The seats in the mess convert to beds, and the spaces under the beds are used for storage, includes the wardroom (officers mess). One such locker in the wardroom is used for the storage of a ready-use quantity of dry ginger ales.

Among the visitors were two very attractive young ladies in their late teens, I would guess, and one was sitting right on top of the dry gingers, which I needed. I asked if she would mind moving over so that I could gain access to the locker; instead, she obliged by parting her legs, so instead of collecting half a dozen bottles, I kept going back for one at a time. Shortly afterwards, one of the officers suggested that I sit down and have a drink, so there I was sitting in the wardroom with one officer and two lovely ladies when Jimmy entered. He took one look at me and went ballistic; it was quite embarrassing at the time (maybe he was jealous). He proceeded to bawl me out, reminding me that I was a junior rating and should keep my place. With this in mind, I left and headed for my own mess, meeting the duty officer on the way. "Get me a drink, Harris, please," he said. "Get it yourself," I replied. "Who's upset you then?" I told him that I didn't mind giving my time, but to be bawled out in front of guests was not on. He said that he would sort it and promptly reported the incident to the Captain, who then gave the Jimmy a rocket and asked me if I would carry on, which I did.

Up until this time, I had had a reasonable relationship with the Jimmy, as with all the officers, but this was the beginning of the end as far as the Jimmy was concerned.

I refused to help out at future functions, and I think he decided to take his revenge over the next few weeks.

We made our way home via the Keil canal, where we were constantly buzzed by Russian MIGS; nothing untoward happened, and we got some good photographs of them.

We were at sea on the surface at night, and I was on watch in the radar office. We had a few contacts on the screen, which I duly reported to the officer of the watch on the bridge, who happened to be the Jimmy. I continued to report as was necessary. "Radar—Bridge do you have a contact bearing green 20?" Not wishing to sound abrupt, I replied "Wait one" (whilst I switched to a longer range and waited for the sweep). "Don't you tell me to wait," he shouted. "What would you like me to say then," I replied. All intercom instructions of this nature are heard by all control room crew, including the Captain in his cabin who at this stage decided to enter the fray with: "Bridge, Radar, this is the Captain, The correct term is '*wait*'." So I duly reported: "Bridge, Radar, wait." The lookout, who was on the bridge at the time, later reported that we had an extra red light glowing brightly on the bridge for some time afterwards.

He then got into the habit of sending or piping for Navigators Yeoman (another of my duties) to the control room at any inconvenient time just to ask me a simple question. On one occasion, I was in the state of undress and took a little longer to get to the control room, and he bawled me out. "I don't care if you turn up with a turd hanging between your legs; when you're sent for, you just get here ."

Watch keeping at sea was one in three. During the day from 0800 to 2000 they were two-hour watches; at night from 2000 to 0800 they were three hours. So if you were lucky, you may get six hours of continuous sleep once every three days when you had the 2000–2300 and 0500–0800. So if one man was unable to keep his watch, it meant three hours on and three hours off.

We had sailed from Gosport on the last day of September, the day before my daughter was born. Shortly afterwards while I was still at sea, on Trafalgar Day, I recall that I wasn't feeling well and obviously didn't look it. I was due to go on watch in the radar office and was prepared to do so, but the lads in the mess didn't think that I was capable, as I was shaking and a little delirious. The Coxswain was called and ordered me to be strapped into my bunk, mainly to stop me from falling out. I recovered after a couple of days and continued my duties as normal for the rest of our time at sea. A week or so later, we returned to Gosport and I was looking forward to going home to see my month-old daughter for the first time. I was sent for by the Jimmy who said that as I was not fit to carry out my duties I was not fit to go ashore. After a heated argument for which I am lucky to have not been reprimanded, I told him that I was going, and I would be requesting to see the Captain the following day. I left the boat and got to the main gate of Dolphin where a message had been left to not let me through. I then went back to the boat, and the navigating officer on the casing was the duty officer. I shouted down to him, "Is the First Lieutenant still on board?" "No." I went down to him and explained the situation, which he claimed to know nothing about. He must have had some idea, because he cleared it for me to go home.

A few more incidents occurred over the next few sessions at sea, one in which I found myself alone on the bridge with him, and he tried to make conversation with me by saying things like "We used to get on so well," etc. "Why are you refusing to speak to me?" "'Cause I don't f***ing like you, and if you don't get off my back, I'll throw you over the f***ing side." He shouted down the voice pipe, "Send a relief lookout to the bridge." I thought I had gone too far, but nothing was said or done.

I had recently developed a very itchy rash all over my body, for which I was receiving treatment from the doctor in Dolphin, to whom I had told the story in case it was related. It turned out to be Pityriasis. The Doc was quite sympathetic and asked me to keep him informed of developments of my relationship with the Jimmy. Things didn't get any better, and I requested to see the Captain to state a complaint. The procedure, if I remember correctly, was that as a request man, you first see the First Lt., who listens to your case and passes you up the line. However, you are not penalized, unlike a defaulter who, whilst waiting to have his case heard, has his leave stopped.

Request men and defaulters were not called until we had returned to Gosport, and as the only request man, I was first to be called. Most of the rest of the crew not on duty had either gone home or inboard. I was asked to state my complaint. As my complaint was against the First Lieutenant, I stated that my request was to see the Captain. "Very well," he said, "The Captain is away for the weekend, and as a Captain's request man, your leave is stopped until you have seen him." "Tell him, Cox'n, he can't do that," I said. The cox'n did; his reply was, "I just did."

"In that case," I said, "I'll see Captain S/M."

"You can," he said, "through the proper channels. First me, then the Captain, then Commander S/M, and next is Captain S/M, and after that, I'll reinstate your leave." I was getting a bit worked up by this time. I don't think the cox'n could believe what was going on. "Right," I said," I know where to find Captain S/M," and I turned round and headed for the fore hatch, up the ladder, and onto the casing towards the gangplank. I think Jimmy had realized he had gone too far—he must have shot up the tower—and he met me on the casing and asked me to calm down, go home for the weekend, and we would speak again on Monday.

Monday came, and he sent for me. "The doctor has suggested you go inboard, as he wants to keep you under observation." This was regarding my rash, which was nearly gone by this time, so to spare crew I was drafted. He did, however, take me to the wardroom gave me a drink and £10 as a parting gift (no hard feelings). Unfortunately, the boat was sailing the following morning and, being spare crew, I was there to slip them. The Captain spotted me from the bridge. "What's that man doing there; get him on board, I need him." We were only away until the weekend and there were no altercations. I was once more drafted to spare crew, where awaited me a draft to the Far East.

AMBUSH

I was given two weeks of foreign draft leave and then given my travel documents and an assurance that I would spend ten months in spare crew, ten months running boat, and ten months refit. As my family was joining me in Singapore, it sounded ideal. My family at this time was my wife, Pat, my son, David, who was two years old, and my daughter, Susan, who was five months old.

I flew from Heathrow, calling at Beirut, Karachi, and Bombay. It only took 24 hours; how things had improved in a few years. It had taken a week on my first flight to Singapore—three days to do the return journey eighteen months later.

On my second day in HMS *Terror* where spare crew was based, I was sent for and told that I was to join HMS *Teredo*. When I questioned why it should be me when there was someone else of the same rating who had already spent nine months in spare crew, I was told that the first lieutenant of the *Teredo* knew me and preferred me. It was the ex Navigating officer, later Jimmy of the *Turpin*. I also learned that the *Teredo* was due to sail back to the UK in a few months time, and an old friend of mine of the same rating who was presently serving on the *Ambush* was down to go with her, so we requested a swap. He would join *Teredo* now, and I would join *Ambush* in his place; this was granted, and then I tried my luck again. The Jimmy of the *Ambush* didn't know me, so why should this other guy not go in my place? The answer was that if the Jimmy of the *Teredo* thought I was preferable, then so did he.

It's a small world as they say. I was recently introduced to an ex submarine officer who lives in the next village; we only spoke on the phone and have yet to meet face to face. However, in conversation we found that we knew a lot of the same people, the Jimmy of the *Teredo* being one of them. Also, that same day I met and spoke to for the first time a lady from the village who turned out to be the daughter of the person with whom I had been speaking—the Jimmy in question was her godfather.

We spent a few days at sea and I arrived back in Singapore to hear that my family was to join me in the next few days. I arranged to rent a house in Johore Bahru, just over the causeway from Singapore into Malaya. They were due to arrive at about 0400 one morning, and I hired a car to meet them at Paya Leba Airport in Singapore. I was dreading telling my wife that once I'd deposited her and the kids at the house, I would have to leave her—as we were sailing at 0800 and would be away for about six weeks. I had arranged for one of the wives to help her settle in, and also arranged for an Ama (servant) which the navy paid for.

A few months later, my five years as a volunteer submariner was up, so I posed the question again—as this same guy was still in spare crew and with my sea time record, was it not fair that we should be swapped? Answer: he wasn't experienced enough. I commented that he never would be at this rate, and as my five years of voluntary service was nearly up, I requested to be transferred back to general service in the next few weeks when my time expired. "Request not granted, we'll keep you for three more years as a non volunteer," he said, as was their right. But to appease me, the other guy was drafted on board so that I could train him and he could gain sea experience. I requested the opportunity to gain some shore time experience, which was ignored—surprise, surprise.

Shortly afterwards, I was sent for and told that my papers had come through for promotion and I was to see the Captain to get it confirmed. I also learned that they had been returned by the Jimmy of the *Trump* six months previously, which had delayed my promotion by six months. So he had had the last laugh, as it cost me dearly financially. I was to carry on doing the same job of second coxswain, but now I would be paid for it.

My bunk was in the torpedo stowage compartment next to what was known as the cabbage patch where fresh vegetables were stored. They wouldn't stay fresh for long and only lasted a few days. But I had this dream that a rat was sitting on my chest, and I woke as I was throwing it away. It turned out to not be a dream, as the next night it was actually in my bed. I was quicker getting out than he was, which was not a pleasant experience; he probably came on board in a bag of spuds or the like. A trap was set, and he was caught the following day.

Our Captain at the time was an excellent tactician, and we were sent to exercise with the American navy around the Philippines to see if we could penetrate a new anti submarine idea of theirs. Apparently they had tried it with a couple of their own boats with great success and wanted to see if we could do any better. I think it was known as the whisky screen, which had nothing to do with drink but rather with the letter W. Five surface ships would take positions on each of the points of the letter W, thus giving them greater coverage whilst searching for us using sonar. They tried for about three days, but couldn't find us even though we kept indicating our position with smoke candles when requested. I'm sure this had a lot to do with our Captain's skill in taking evasive action; maybe he'd gained his experience on mystery trips similar to those of my own. Once ashore in Manila when we met members of the crews of the American ships, we were welcomed as heroes for reasons unknown. I am still baffled to this day—perhaps they were just being magnanimous in defeat.

We would then have sailed to Hong Kong and on to Japan before making our return trip back to Singapore, once again calling in at Hong Kong on the way, exercising with various ships of American, British, Australian, and New Zealand navies.

There was always plenty to catch up on whilst at home in Malaya. I'd bought a motorbike for travelling to and from the boat based alongside HMS *Medway*, our depot ship, close to the naval base HMS *Terror.* I also used it for collecting fish and chips from our nearest chip shop at Serangoon in Singapore 17 miles away. My sister was also living there at the time, as her husband was serving with the RAF.

It was policy that if you ran over one of the many chickens running loose in the road, you didn't stop for fear of being lynched; the same rule applied if it was a human being. The only difference was that you had to report the incident to the nearest police station. Fortunately, I never had that problem. The bike was also very useful for going to the local market to hire a car, which I did regularly when at home. We used to travel up to a lovely beach that I discovered by studying the navigation charts, known as Jason's Bay. It was almost deserted when we first visited except for a couple of locals; it soon became known and very popular. I understand that it is now a holiday resort.

We lived in one of twelve semi detached bungalows; making a small estate with no proper road to it. It was built on part of the area where the film *A Town Like Alice* was filmed. I think the only piece of tarmac was the drive leading off a rough track to our pair of bungalows. The drive was between the front of our home and the homes in front of us where a friend of mine who was serving on the *Andrew* lived with his wife. There was one other submariner living on the estate, plus a couple of general service families. The rest were a mixture of nationalities— Italian, Chinese, Malay, and Indian. We all got on really well. My immediate neighbour was a Malay named Mokhtar with a Chinese wife who had taken the western name of Elsie, both in government, and they had an Indian lodger, Devaganum, who was a doctor. On many occasions, we all went out for a meal together. If I was home when Mok arrived home from work, he would throw his car keys into our house and shout, "The car's yours for the night."

Around each pair of bungalows was an open gully where water from the kitchen sink, shower, washbasins, and rainwater would run before it went to the soak away or monsoon drain. When we did go out for the night, on our return, we could see rats the size of cats under the slabs covering the gully by the doorways. I decided to get rid of them. I took a gallon of petrol and poured it into the drain while running water from the sink. When I thought the house was surrounded, I threw in a match; the two houses were surrounded by fire and there were a few fire balls running into the wilderness.

Shortly afterwards, pleased with my success, I was sitting in the garden of my friend from the *Andrew* when I spotted a rat looking out of one of the many holes in the bank supporting my drive. Out came the petrol and a piece of tubing, and by siphoning the petrol and holding a thumb over the end, we poked the tube into the holes and released a trail of petrol. When I threw in a match this time we must have killed a few rats, but it also blew up my drive; we had permanent speed bumps after that.

Pat and I were sitting on a wall at the bottom of our drive talking to friends when she leapt up, screamed, and ran for the house. I followed to discover that she was frantically stripping off her shorts and pants and running the shower; apparently she literally did have ants in her pants. On another occasion, our son had wandered to that same spot, which effectively was a bridge over the monsoon drain, and fell into the drain. Fortunately, it was dry at the time, and our doctor neighbour was at home and able to treat his injuries. However, David, being David, was soon out and about again, and within an hour he had done exactly the same thing again.

It was always a policy to inspect the bath before jumping in, as it was a place that the bootlace snakes liked as well. They were called bootlace because that's precisely what they look like; they were supposedly deadly and tended to climb from the gully up the waste pipe and into the bath. It was also common to find snakes in the garden. I heard about many other people's experiences with snakes, but I can't recall anyone being bitten by one. In the seas around Malaya, we used to see hundreds of sea snakes, always in pairs on the surface; many times, when preparing to enter harbour, we found them trapped amongst the mooring cables secured below the casing. A couple of the lads took to skinning them and making belts out of them.

Of all of the boats that I served on, I only came across one episode of stealing, and this was on the *Ambush*. It spoiled what was otherwise a very happy atmosphere; people's personal valuables were being taken from the boat as well as from our inboard locker room in HMS *Terror*. I happened to walk into the locker room one lunch time and heard an argument going on; they were oblivious to my presence. One of the lads was a friend of mine. He had apparently caught the thief red-handed with his money and couldn't prove it, and he was saying, "If you hand over my money, I won't say anything." When he agreed, I made my presence known and said, "I don't care what you've agreed; if you don't report him, I'll report both of you." The offender was reported and punished, and he never returned to the boat.

On one occasion a few weeks before I came home, I arranged to borrow the launch nicknamed *The African Queen* from the Medway, to take some of the families of crew members and our neighbours on a trip down the Straits of Johore to one of the islands. We took the barbecue, lots of food and drink, and a single homemade water ski, which a few of us took in turns to try out on the outward journey. By the time we arrived at our destination, some of us had gotten the hang of it. Once we had everyone ashore and the food was eaten, we decided to get some more ski practice in; after I had my turn, I was struggling to get back on board when I was suddenly reminded that the boat was fitted with Kitchener gear. This is the system in which the screw turns constantly and is fitted with what are known as buckets, devices that can be opened and closed around the screw. If the rear end is open, the boat is propelled forward; if the front end is opened, the boat goes in reverse. The wider open it is, the higher the speed, and sometimes the propulsion is neither forward nor backward. Hanging onto the side of the boat, I had lowered myself further into the water to get more momentum to pull myself up, but my legs were sucked under the boat towards the screw. Once I realised what was happening I pulled up rather rapidly and tried further forward, but I came very close to losing a foot.

The boat was fitted with an awning, and most of my passengers were shaded by this on both the outbound and inbound journeys, but as I was steering the thing, I was out in the sun constantly in just my swim suit. We'd left at around sunrise, 0700, and arrived home just after sunset, so I'd spent twelve full hours in very hot sun. I swore on the night that the moon was green, and a couple of days later I shed my brown skin completely. I never really got my tan back to go home with.

All good things come to an end, and we were due for a mystery trip, this time off China, so here we go again. We had been on patrol for about two weeks when the main periscope flooded. The submarine has two periscopes: the main or search periscope and the attack periscope. Unfortunately, the attack periscope is not designed to be used whilst snorting (too much vibration), so we were unable to recharge our batteries whilst submerged. As we were a long way from home and in hostile waters, we had no choice but to surface and run for it. We adopted what is known as patrol routine; everything was opened up for diving and Q tank flooded, making us low in the water and also helping us to get down quickly when necessary, which was quite frequently. We had two lookouts on the bridge and Shuff Duff listening, and as soon as anything was sighted or racket was heard by Shuff Duff, down we would go.

We did have a few close encounters; one was with an intelligence trawler that was travelling with no lights at night, and another with a MIG that came from nowhere. As he was not using radar, we didn't pick him up until he was visible. If he had been using radar, we would have heard him on the Shuff Duff; they certainly knew we were there. Once we were in international waters, we breathed a sigh of relief and headed for Singapore. Most of us thought that would be it, home to base and, for some, to our families. We arrived alongside *Medway* and we were swamped with top brass and experts to look at the periscope. We were allowed on the *Medway* but no further; two marines were stationed at the gangway leading ashore. A few of us contemplated getting into *Medway*'s launch, which was tied up along the side nearest the shore, slipping the rope, and letting the tide take us clear. Then we could make for the opposite shore, which was Malaya, and head home. Fortunately, the tide was flowing in the wrong direction, as we would have been washed onto the pontoons forming a bridge to the shore, right under the marines' noses. Even if it hadn't been flowing the wrong direction, I don't think we would have done it; it was just a mind exercise. Things were tense; we had had a rough time and we didn't know what was going on. We were looking for things to occupy our minds. We then decided to wind the Coxswain up. We each had a jug of orange and produced a couple of cans of metal polish and pretended that we were the worse for wear, drinking a lethal alcoholic cocktail. However, he knew how to handle us. If he had tried to get us all to do something together, we would have just sat there; instead he ordered us individually. Refusal would have been a direct disobedience of order, a serious offence. It wasn't long before he realized it was a wind up.

In the early hours of the following morning, the periscope had been fixed, and the decision was made that we would go back and carry on where we left off—so off we went with more than a little trepidation. The periscope held up, and the mission went without unusual problems; we ended up a few weeks later in Hong Kong for a two-week break.

Whenever possible, when a submarine is in harbour they try to accommodate the crew, either in barracks or depot ship, but as there were no vacancies we were initially accommodated in the YMCA in Kowloon, on the Chinese mainland. We complained that this was very basic, so we were given living and ration allowance and left to find our own digs of which there was a wide variety, depending on choice and morals. I chose the China Fleet club, central to most things going on.

One of the sonar units that we had on board was the same as that first installed on the *Turpin*. It could pick up the propeller noise of a ship over a hundred miles away; however, because it was so sensitive, it would also pick up any noise made on the boat. Therefore, whilst this was in operation, everything was shut down—freezer, pumps, and, in this climate when we most needed the air conditioning, all motors shut down except one main motor that turned just enough to keep control of the depth and steerage. Under these conditions, all we could do if not on watch was lie on our bunks and sweat it out for the few hours that it would take to complete a few sweeps. The practice was, as the transducers were situated on each side of the boat and not directional (because the noise created by a motor to drive them would drown any contact), the boat would travel in a circle, and any contacts would be logged, then another circle, and another, each time logging the contacts. This way their course and speed could be estimated. On one occasion, we had some experts on board to monitor the effectiveness of the equipment and the conditions that it created for the crew. We spent a week on these trials; at one time, the one guy told us that the humidity was over 97 percent, and he commented that with another 3 percent, we would be swimming. After the week, he gloated that after such a hard time they were awarded a week's recuperation leave, unlike us; we were to spend another two weeks at sea.

We had a new member of crew who had recently arrived from the UK, and his wife was due to join him; I volunteered to take him to the airport to meet her. As she was due to arrive at 0400, I suggested that he stay with us overnight.

As we drove down the hill into Johore Baru, there was a level crossing and I could see a car's headlights flashing at me, so I slowed down. It was a police car, and as the policeman approached I could see behind him what looked like a 16 feet by 1foot log. He said that we had a python that had had his breakfast and decided to sleep it off between the gates of the level crossing, and they were waiting for help to remove it. I explained the urgency of our journey, and he suggested that if he pushed the gates back parallel with the lines maybe I could squeeze past it. This I did, but it was a bit worrying as there was only room on the tarmac for the wheels on the left side of the car—the other two had to bounce over the rails. When we returned, about two hours later, there was no sign of the snake.

Around this time we had a change of Captain and set off for Australia via the Bali straits. At the time, we were having problems with President Sukarno over Borneo. From the time of leaving Singapore we had to be prepared for trouble, so we opened up for diving and stayed at patrol routine until we were through the Bali Straits and clear of Indonesian waters. Then it was exercises with the Australian and New Zealand navies, and during these exercises we had what every submariner dreads: a fire on board. I used to sleep in the torpedo stowage compartment just forward of the main accommodation space, and I was woken by a lot of shouting. When submerged for long periods of time, the air gets rather stale, short of oxygen and high in CO_2, and when the match won't stay alight long enough to light a cigarette, a remedy is needed. We had two CO_2 absorption units, generally known as abortion units, and two oxygen generators, one of each at each end of the boat. The forward ones were placed in the seamen's mess. The abortion unit had four changeable canisters which the air was sucked through for four hours before being changed. The oxygen generator required what was known as a candle, which was a solid cylindrical slug of material about 15 inches long by 4 inches in diameter. I jumped out of my bunk, as I could see smoke coming from the accommodation space, then heard over the intercom, "Control room - accommodation space, there's a lot of smoke in here and a lot of people are choking!" I shouted to the fore ends watch keeper to get me the breathing apparatus, then I heard someone choke, "The Bunting's bed's on fire!" so without waiting for the breathing equipment, I foolishly ran into the smoke to help, or see what type of extinguisher was needed. The bunting had already left for the control room along with everyone else; his bed was on fire where the oxygen generator had developed a fault, and the melted candle had oozed out and set the bedding on fire. During this time, instructions had been given to fire a red grenade to warn ships above that we were making an emergency surface, along with orders of full ahead, full rise on planes, and blow all main ballast. Once on the surface, the hatches were kept closed, for fear of feeding the fire with oxygen, until we had extinguished the fire. I suffered with a very sore chest for a while after that, but I don't seem to have suffered any long term damage. We eventually made our way to Sydney where we spent a couple of happy weeks except for one night. We were accommodated and fed in the Australian naval barracks, and I woke up to the sound of someone throwing up and then realized there was more than one, and suddenly it was my turn. I hadn't had a drink that night so it wasn't that; if I had been drunk, it wouldn't have been so painful. What was coming up was almost solid, and I feared I might choke as I couldn't clear it. About a dozen of us reported to the sick bay in the morning, but no common cause could be pinpointed, and none of us felt ill.

We left Sydney for Townsville in North Queensland, with a brief call at Wellington, New Zealand.

On our way back to Singapore, the Captain sent for me. He was a Scotsman and I really liked this man and got on really well with him. He asked if we had an inflatable dinghy, as his inventory said we should have. "Yes," I said. "Has it been tested recently?" he asked. "No sir." "Well it's time it was, get it ready; we'll try it out in an hour's time." We were getting close to Indonesian waters again so we were in patrol routine. We manhandled the kit onto the casing and inflated it. "Don't bother with struggling to get it into the water," he said, "lay it on the casing, and the two of you just sit in it and I'll dive the boat," which he did, and we floated away. I saw the periscope pop up, so we were being watched—then it disappeared, and believe me it was very eerie. There was no land in sight, no ships, just the vast ocean. He left us there for about half an hour; he may have sighted us through the periscope, but I didn't see it. Then he surfaced about a hundred yards away. We had to paddle over to the boat, and on the way Sam said, "I bet he dives again just before we get there." But he didn't. That was the only time in 2 ½ years that the dinghy touched the water. He had another mad idea for me on another occasion; he wanted photographs of the boat diving and suggested that I sit on top of the radar mast with the camera. The mast would then be raised, and he would dive the boat, and I was to take up to twelve pictures on the way down and again as we surfaced. I felt safe as I didn't think he would want his camera ruined. The results were quite good. I did have a couple of copies, but they are lost with so much of my other memorabilia.

One day whilst in Singapore, a few of the lads arranged to meet at a bar in Sembawang Village, not far from the naval base to celebrate something. Because I knew I would be drinking, I used a taxi to get there. I don't remember anything worth mentioning about the night, but because I needed a taxi to take me home, my friend Bill Sagaar, who had ridden to the bar on his scooter and lived with his family in Serangoon, gave me a lift to the roundabout where the taxis waited for fares. The following morning, Bill didn't show up, and no one had seen or heard from him. Later that day we found out why. He was found dead in a monsoon ditch; he'd choked to death on his own vomit, which he couldn't excrete whilst travelling. It seemed that I was the last person to see him alive.

Having been on exercise with some of our own ships off the coast of Malaya, the ships all anchored off the Island of Pulau Tioman. We tied up alongside the cruiser HMS *Belfast*, now berthed near Tower Bridge as a museum. We'd wandered off from the beach where we were to be picked up. Making our way back round a headland in the water I realised that I'd lost my new waterproof Longines watch. I donned one of the sets of snorkels we'd taken with us and started retracing our steps as it were, not really expecting to find it, but luck was with me. I was just about to give up when I spotted it face up amongst the coral. That was 1962, and I still have it working today.

On one of our repeat excursions to the Philippines, Hong Kong, Japan, and back, we were once again involved in exercises with various navies, and at the end of it a helicopter was supplying us with fresh provisions. I was on the bridge, as usual, unhooking each load, being lifted off my feet as the boat rose up and down in the swell. When the last of the stores had been deposited, the Captain said, "Hang on to that hook, we have some records to go back." I wish he had told the helicopter pilot the same thing, because I was lifted off and it was too late to let go. The first the helicopter crew knew that they had an extra passenger was when I arrived alongside the open door, God knows how many feet in the air. They quickly turned around and I was lowered back on to the boat; I don't know where I found the strength to hang on for what seemed like an eternity. As I dropped onto the boat, the hook was caught, the records hooked on, and the chopper was gone, leaving me with my aching muscles.

We finally returned to Singapore for a couple of weeks before setting off for Pakistan; we joined the fleet on the way for exercises. After the exercises, we were to be supplied with fresh stores from one of the larger ships and also receive mail from home. A boat was sent across to us and came alongside by the fore planes; the sea was a bit choppy, and the boat was bouncing around some, making it difficult to pass the stores from them to us. Their boat was fitted with Kitchener gear as previously described, and one of my team fell into the water between their boat and us. Recalling my previous experience, I jumped into their boat and shut off the engine. Later that day, I was describing some ideas I'd been having since the incident for a much safer way of transferring stores and men. A couple of the guys, Topsy Turner being one of them, expressed their reservations and said, "You'll never get me on it." It was in general use between ship to ship, similar to the Breeches Buoy, but a submarine has no high point and is somewhat limited for space to have many men hauling on ropes. A couple of days later, the Captain sent for me and said he'd heard of my idea, and suggested I run through it with him.

We eventually arrived in Karachi and berthed alongside one of their cruisers that we had sold to them, and they had renamed the *Mysore*. This ship, I believe, was originally HMS *Nigeria*, the ship on which I had spent two weeks training aboard in Rosythe as a sea cadet. I was only thirteen at the time, and up till then, because of the war and sweet rationing that was still in force at the time, sweets and chocolate had been a rarity in my life, and to find that we could buy as much as we liked was too much of a temptation. When I eventually arrived home, I had my small attaché case full of Cadbury's Dairy Milk, which made me very popular with both family and friends for a while.

The first thing that the crew wanted to do on arriving alongside the *Mysore* was go for a shower; as I had work to do, I decided to wait until the rush had died down before walking across the gang plank with my towel around my neck. I was greeted by a dozen or so of their crew, and their leader explained that they were not too happy with how our lads had gone into their bathroom, stripped off, and showered in full view of each other; in fact, it offended them. I was told what I must do, and to pass the word to the rest of the crew for future reference. Keep your clothes on whilst you brush your teeth, then step into the shower cubicle before undressing and hang your clothes outside, shower and dry yourself, get dressed before leaving the cubicle. It seemed a complete waste of time to me, as whilst I was in the shower they were fighting to get a look at me naked. I did pass on the message, however, and added that it might be wise to go in a group.

We put to sea to exercise with the Pakistan Navy and exchanged half a dozen crew members with the same number from one of their destroyers for the experience; this was during Ramadan when they are not allowed to eat or drink during daylight hours. Tot time came and they declined, so we drank theirs, then came lunch. I felt sorry for them, as they obviously wanted to join us. Then one of them said, "How deep are we?" I said, "120 feet." "We'll eat," he said. "He won't see us down here." Later that day, the Captain sent for me again. "Are you sure this transfer idea of yours will work?" "In theory, yes sir." "Okay; when we surface we'll arrange for our lads on board the destroyer to be transferred back, and we'll send their crew back the same way, so get the kit sorted and liaise with those who need to know. I'll want you on the bridge to take charge of the operation, and the torpedo officer will be in charge of the men below manning the lines." I did his bidding and also conferred with the gun layer, who would use a rifle to fire a rod and line across to the destroyer. My idea was to use the equipment carried for emergency tow ship combined with the other ship's equipment for transfer at sea, with a few modifications. The destroyer came abreast of us about 30 metres away, the gun layer fired his line, and before long we had all of the equipment in place. A sack of potatoes was sent across first as a test, and then the first of our exchange crew was detailed. I gave Topsy a big grin as he arrived; he said, "Well done," and shook my hand. The whole operation went smoothly, except that as I was passing the orders and the Jimmy was relaying them to the torpedo officer below, I could hear the Jimmy repeating my order of "Check, Check," (i.e., slacken the rope), and I could hear the voice of the torpedo officer coming up through the tower shouting "Heave." This could have caused an accident, so I went over to the voice pipe and shouted "Check, you stupid *******!" The Jimmy was none too pleased with me for speaking to an officer in such a manner, but the skipper pointed out that he had put me in charge, and he endorsed my comment. We used this method of transfer frequently thereafter, and it was adopted as standard procedure on all submarines; the last I heard, it was still in use. The Captain got the praise from the admiralty, of course, but then it's always the captain that is held responsible when things go wrong, as would have happened if this exercise had gone bad, so I suppose that's fair.

One of the Fleet auxiliary ship's Captains took up the idea and tried to improve on it; it was tried out on us, but unfortunately it was unsuccessful, which was a pity as it would have reduced the submarine crew's involvement.

Whilst on one of our visits to Japan—Yokohama and Yokosuka were now our main ports of call—we were billeted in the American naval base. Before spending too much money on life's pleasures, the rabbit run took priority(buying presents to take back home to the family). George and I spent the afternoon doing just this and then called in at one of the many bars in what was known as submarine ally, where all the American submariners drank. You didn't buy drink in these bars (that we bought in one of the many shops), all you bought was the ice and food. If you didn't finish your bottle, you marked the level, put your name on it, and left it behind the bar until next time. We hadn't been there long when a voice said "You blooming English, you didn't even know I'd taken your bottle." It was a big a black American, Emanuel Hunter from San Diego— also a submariner. He helped us finish our bottle, then went to the bar and picked his own and one of the bottles that had been left by one of his friends. The following morning, one of the lads said he'd seen us with this American in another bar, and someone else said we were seen in a different bar. I remembered leaving the original bar in daylight, and on reflection I remembered getting back to our billet in the dark, but the intervening hours are gone for good. Later that morning we had a visitor on the boat: Emanuel Hunter. We offered him coffee. "Coffee; when

I'm with the blooming English, I only drink blooming tea." Apparently he had been based in London for a while and tried very much to speak like an English gentleman when it suited. He spent a lot of time in our company. It seemed that he preferred it to that of his own shipmates; being the only black person on board may have been the reason.

One night before returning to our accommodation, we called in one of the Japanese takeaways where some of his white countrymen were also waiting in the queue, along with many of our crew. Some Americans made it clear that they didn't like blacks and were quite insulting to him. He was big enough to look after himself, but we made it clear to them that we didn't like their attitude and that if it got physical, it wouldn't be just him that they were taking on. As we outnumbered them, they quietened down, and we eventually left with our food and Emanuel.

We never did return to Kure, so I didn't get the chance to look up my ex girlfriend; six years had gone by, and if Kure had altered as much as other places I'd visited, I would have had difficulty finding her.

We did call in for a few days at the Japanese island of Okinawa, another American base, then on the way back to Hong Kong whilst dived we could hear a scraping noise with an occasional bang, like something was loose. The Captain sent for me and asked my opinion, as I was responsible for the outside of the boat. I said that everything was secure before I came below but did admit that it sounded like the plank was moving about. He decided to surface and investigate; myself and my assistant, Sam, would be required to take a closer look if necessary. My suspicion turned out to be correct. The weather was quite rough, so we each wore a harness attached to a length of rope, the end of which we clipped to the guard rail (a wire rope attached between stantions). We discovered that one of the bolts holding the plank down had sheared, and another was looking the worse for wear. I sent below for a rope and set about trying to secure it. With the job in hand, we couldn't tie ourselves too close to the guard rail, and because of the rough weather we had difficulty keeping our feet on the casing, as the waves were washing over us and sweeping us off the boat, I remember on a couple of occasions being swept to one side, only to be picked up by the next wave and thrown completely over to the other side, and I watched the same happen to Sam. We did manage to get the plank secured and took our soggy bruised bodies down below, where the Captain arranged for a tot of rum for us both.

On entering Hong Kong waters in the early hours, the sea as usual was a mass of Junks. The trouble was that they didn't show any lights until you were almost upon them, so it was always a little traumatic. On this occasion, I was on the bridge as lookout with the OOW, and I reported a ship dead ahead showing both green and red lights, along with its white masthead light indicating that it was heading straight for us. Then I realised it couldn't be one ship as the green and red lights were the wrong way round, and I mentioned this to the OOW; then the lights started to draw apart, confirming that it was two different ships, and the OOW altered course to go between them. Then, to my horror, I saw that it was one ship, the American aircraft carrier *Kitty Hawk*. What we had mistaken as a red port navigation light was a red hangar light, and we were heading between that and its green Starboard navigation light. The order, "Hard a port and full astern," stopped us from colliding with her. The signalman was sent for and we tried to make contact but got no response; their lookouts obviously didn't look behind them.

We were looking forward to returning to Singapore, as we were due to take the boat into a much needed refit, so my last four months would be ashore, going home three nights out of four to my family. As usual with my luck, plans were changed; we were detailed for another ten-week trip to Pakistan, exercising with our own fleet on the way and the same routine as before. But this time we were limited to a diving depth of 150 feet and had to surface every couple of hours to pump out the water, as it was coming in faster than we could pump it out. The engineer officer fought very hard to get this trip cancelled, as he didn't think the boat was safe. I learned later that he had so little faith in us surviving that when he said goodbye to his wife, he really meant it. I'm here to tell the story, so we obviously did make it, but it was something of a nightmare and an embarrassment.

On returning to Singapore, I had six weeks left before my 2.5 years were up. We spent this time getting her into dry dock and stripping her out for refit. Whilst someone was dismantling the emergency flap valve, it was discovered that it was very badly corroded, so much so that it broke off in the guy's hand.

When snorting, if for any reason the upper valve doesn't stop the water coming in, the inrush of water automatically closes the emergency flap valve, which would have happened when we took our unscheduled plunge on the *Turpin*. This gives the engine room time to shut the induction hull valve. We have never really known what happened when the *Affray* was lost, but it is believed that her snort mast was snapped off, and this valve could have saved her if it had been working.

It was whilst we were in Singapore on one occasion that I met up with Tony again from the *Trespasser*; I had met him here previously as he was serving on the *Andrew*. I'd gone to the fleet club in Terror one lunchtime and met him at the bar, which surprised me, as the last time we met he was still teetotal. He had lined up four pints. When I questioned this, he said, "There's one for every year of abstinence." Unfortunately, it didn't stop at four, as I heard later. Later that afternoon, Tony's wife was outside their house being invited by one of their neighbours to a party that night. As she was explaining that she and her husband didn't drink, a taxi pulls up and out falls Tony and he throws up on the lawn. I didn't hear what happened afterwards, but I met up with him again on another boat back in the UK, and he was still married to the same girl and still drinking.

Two days before I was due to fly back to the UK, I was sent home to get my kit and wait for transport to pick me up and take me over to Changi. From there, I was to be flown by helicopter out to sea to join submarine *Amphion* to relieve someone who had been taken off sick. Fortunately, one of our kindly officers knew my history and thought this was one unfairness too many and fought my case. The first I knew of this was when the transport turned up and I was told that someone else was being drafted instead, and to report for duty for my last day on the *Ambush*.

In the 2.5 years, we visited most of these places at least twice. Andaman Islands, Karachi, Pulau Tioman, Hong Kong (regularly), Yokohama, Yokosuka, Okinawa, Manila, Subic Bay, Sangley Point, Langkawi, Singapore, Borneo, Port Blaire, Sydney, Wellington, and Townsville NQL.

We flew home together as a family. We almost left without our daughter Susan—who was now nearly three years old—as whilst we were saying our goodbyes and boarding the taxi, the Ama was still holding her in her arms.

TOKEN

On arriving home, with about fourteen months left to serve and about nine weeks FS (foreign service) leave, I decided to buy the house that I had saved and planned for. A lot of this organising was eventually left to my wife, as after five weeks I had a telegram saying, "Join Submarine Token on arrival in Gosport," and gave the date, a few days hence.

Once again, I said my goodbyes and reported to Dolphin and joined *Token*. However, I was not allowed to sail with her; my escape training was out of date, as we have to re-qualify every three years, so I had to stay for the week and re-qualify in the escape training tank. Meanwhile, according to the crew, she had made her way to Londonderry, Northern Ireland, where she was to be based for a while. However, my travel documents said that I should travel to Faslane and join her. I questioned this with the drafting Chief who asked, "Are you trying to tell me how to do my job? On your bike or, better still, train." On arrival at Faslane, surprise, surprise, she's not here she's over in Derry. Another train journey to Stranrar, ferry to Belfast, and train to Londonderry.

Whilst I was in the Far East, the leave situation had changed. Someone had realised that if our enemy wanted to attack us, Xmas, Easter, or the summer holiday would be a good time, so instead of the submarine service part closing down three times a year, cycle leave was introduced, meaning Xmas leave could be for each boat any time between September and March, and Easter leave would be between January and June, etc. So, having lost some of my FS leave, one of my first questions was, "When is Xmas leave?" "Sorry we've had ours." " How about me?" "Tough."

Everyone remembers where they were when Kennedy was shot. I was with a couple of mates on shore leave and we'd gone over the border. As we came out of a bar, we were confronted by a policeman who broke the news to us and suggested that we return back over the border lest someone decide to take out their rage on us.

It was a few days later that we were preparing to go to sea. I was part of the casing party (those of us who in all sorts of weather are responsible for untying us from the jetty or depot ship, and securing the outside of the boat for sea, and of course tying us up when we returned). We had singled up (removed all but the fore and aft lines securing us), and were waiting for the Captain to come aboard, at which time we would take in the plank, secure it, and let go of the fore and aft lines. The Jimmy came to me and said, "If you want your Xmas leave and you can get changed and off the boat before the Captain arrives, you can go." It was a little bit like Robin Hood and Little John, as the Captain and I met in the middle of the plank; I did the honourable thing and retreated—then I was going one way as the plank was going the other, but I made it. That was the day that Kennedy was buried. I travelled to Belfast and caught the overnight ferry to Liverpool and the train to Birmingham and my newly bought house.

It was in January that I was on weekend leave, due to leave to catch my train on Sunday evening back to Gosport, when I felt like I had been stabbed in the stomach. The pain subsided but returned every few minutes, so my wife called the doctor, who decided I was not fit to travel. My wife then went next door to use the telephone, as we had not yet been connected, and reported the situation. I was allowed to travel after a couple of days with the doc saying, "I think you have appendicitis, but as you would normally feel unwell with it, and you don't, I suspect it is twisted."

I was examined in Dolphin and kept inboard for observation, as I had no symptoms. Two days later, I literally crawled into the sick bay and was rushed into Haslar Hospital; my appendix was removed, and as my home doctor had suspected, it had been tangled. I was eventually discharged with a week's sick leave. I remember travelling home on a bitterly cold day with 2–3 inches of snow. By the time I arrived at Birmingham New Street Station, I wasn't feeling well at all and doubled up in considerable pain. I managed to get on the bus and arrive at my destination, which was a few hundred yards from my home. By the time I had walked there, I couldn't reach the door bell, so I lay on the doorstep banging the bottom of the door, where my wife found me. She immediately rang for the doctor, who fortunately came straight round to discover that I had developed a haematoma. This laid me up for a while. After my leave had expired, the doctor came to see me whilst I was still confined to bed and asked if I thought I was fit to go back to sea, as my Jimmy had rung him and told him to send me back as the boat was going to sea tomorrow. Apparently his reply had been, "Do you want me to supply a body bag as well?"

RORQUAL

When I returned to Dolphin, the *Token* was still at sea, but there was another one waiting for me—the *Rorqual*, with a Canadian Captain. I was to relieve someone of identical rate who was going off to do a PO's course, which was something that I had been recommended for on numerous occasions over the past three years but no one would let me go. So I was not too pleased at this draft, apart from meeting up with some old mates, Tony being one of them.

We visited Lorient in France and were billeted in the French naval barracks. Tony and I went ashore together; I couldn't speak a word of French, and Tony had what he called a schoolboy grasp of the language. He ordered the drinks, two beers and two pastis. I managed two or three of this combination, then declined the pastis; Tony managed to keep drinking both. The more he drank, the more fluent in French he became, and by the time we were ready to get back to the boat, we'd made a few friends. Two of them offered us a lift back to the boat in their CV3, which we accepted. By the time we got back to the dockyard, Tony was out of it, and I had great difficulty getting the driver to take us to our billet and not the boat. They helped me get Tony inside. I had the bottom bunk and Tony the top, but I decided it was easier to put Tony in mine, and I had the top. I thanked our newly found friends and bid them farewell. Tony's job, apart from also being radar, was chief's mess man; he would collect their food, serve it, and clear up afterwards.

The following morning, I woke early as usual and looked down to see if Tony was up, as he had to get back on board since we were still eating on the boat. He looked a disgusting mess and had vomited and urinated; he and the floor were covered. He was still in his uniform, as we hadn't bothered to undress him; that was covered as well, and his beard was matted with vomit. I managed to rouse him, and he dutifully got up and staggered off, I thought to get cleaned up. It wasn't long before he returned in the same state and said "The chiefs don't want breakfast this morning." One look at him would have turned the strongest of stomachs.

The memorable part of being on this boat was an incident after there had been a typhoid outbreak somewhere in the UK. On inspection, it was discovered that we had on board some of the suspect contaminated tins of corned beef. We were doing some day running from Faslane so we were back alongside most nights for runs ashore, and on discovery of the suspect meat, as a lot of us were feeling under the weather, we were all suspect cases. Those who did feel okay were allowed ashore but told not to broadcast our situation. Anyway someone did, and the first our families knew of our plight was when we made the headlines on the TV evening news, with film of us sailing up Gareloch that had the caption "Quarantined Sub." After that we were quarantined, and we all recovered from our illnesses (hangovers). During our quarantine, my relief returned from his course, but because of our quarantine I wasn't allowed to leave the boat.

Our dress on board was usually fairly casual and I never wore any badges. I was occupying the bunk previously occupied by the man I had relieved, and now that he had returned he demanded his bunk back. I told him what to do, to which he said, "I'm giving you a direct order to vacate my bunk!" I repeated my previous answer. "That's it," he said, "get your cap!" Off we went to see the Coxswain. "I'm running this man in for direct disobedience of orders." "You can't do that," said the Coxswain. "He's senior to you." He didn't have to suffer for long, as I was drafted back to Dolphin a couple of days later when the quarantine was lifted.

PORPOISE

I hadn't spent long in spare crew before I was drafted to my last boat, the *Porpoise*. Once again, we spent a lot of time running from Faslane and Derry. On one occasion in Derry, we were recalled from shore leave one night, as an unidentified submarine had been seen in the Irish Sea. We put to sea to help locate her. I was on the bridge as one of the lookouts whilst Radar had a contact two miles directly astern of us; we started to do a 360 degree turn and still this contact was two miles astern of us, and I got suspicious. I looked at the masts that we had up, Radar and radio, and said to the officer of the watch, "I think we have a false echo, or that contact can really move fast." "What do you mean?" he asked. "Well, if we have turned 360 degrees in a circle of about one mile at a speed of 12 knots and he has stayed two miles astern of us, he must have travelled about 40 miles or more in the same time." He didn't answer, so I said, "I can make it disappear, sir." "How?" "Lower the radio mast." He gave the order, "Lower ALE." Then from the Radar office, "Contact disappeared." I'd come across this problem before; we were getting a back echo off the radio mast. We never did locate the unidentified boat, no doubt a Russian doing to us what we so often did to them. I remember on the *Turpin* whilst we were in the Barents sea, the OOW was looking through the periscope and spotted a Russian submarine going in the opposite direction to us. I remember commenting that we could have stayed off Portland to meet her.

Whilst at a depth of 150 feet, a shout was heard from the officer's steward, "There's water pouring in here!" We immediately surfaced and the faulty valve was repaired. On another occasion, I had just completed the middle watch (0200–0500) and the boat was to do a maximum safety depth dive shortly afterwards, so I decided to stay awake for this. Being one of the newer boats, she was built for a safety depth of 1000 feet. I didn't have to wait long; as soon we were on our way down, the boat started to creak as the outside pressure came on. Suddenly, there was a rush of air as main ballasts were blown, and we were on our way up again. As key personnel take over watches, certain checks have to be made; I learned afterwards that as one engineer was descending a ladder into a machinery space, three rungs down his feet hit water. The boat was flooding. He shouted to the control room and the boat did an emergency surface from 600 feet. If much more water had been taken on, we would never have been able to surface; we would have carried on down until we hit the bottom.

We paid a visit to Esbjerg in Denmark, and my last port of call was Hull. There the local hospital had laid on a dance for us and for the nurses; a good time was had by all, and a few new relationships started. Then it was back to Gosport in time for me to do a two-week rehabilitation course before I left for good.

Even after I'd started my course, I was recalled and told I had gotten another draft; the fact that the boat wasn't due back until after my time had expired didn't seem to matter. I managed to get out of this one. Then they had the cheek to ask me to sign on, with a promise of a PO's course and the next Radar course, a promise which would have lasted until I had signed the dotted line. I decided that living like a sardine (covered in oil and packed into a tin can) was no longer for me. I declined.

Having had this experience, I think that I may have the solution for world peace. If the politicians or warring factions could hold their "Peace" negotiations in an old "S," "T," or "A" class submarine (or even earlier type), at sea, and that conference were made to last at least eight weeks, with two weeks spent on the surface in rough weather, they would learn to make peace or kill each other; either would produce the same result.

A RECORD OF SUBMARINE SERVICE

November1956:   Start submarine training
March 1957:   Join S/m *Turpin*
January 1960:   Leave *Turpin* for hospital
February 1960:   Return from sick leave, join S/m *Trespasser*
April 1960:   Leave *Trespasser*, join spare crew
April 1960:   Rejoin S/m *Turpin* for one week
April 1960:   Leave *Turpin* to spare crew
April 1960:   Join S/m *Aeneas*
One Saturday morning July 1960:
                         Leave *Aeneas*, join spare crew, rejoin *Turpin*
                         Leave *Turpin*, rejoin spare crew, join S/m *Trump*
March 1961:   Leave *Trump* to spare crew, rejoin *Trump* for one week
March 1961   Draft to Far East (Singapore)
March 1961:   Draft to *Teredo* / swapped / Joined S/m *Ambush*
September 1963:   Leave *Ambush* / Draft to S/m *Amphion* cancelled
October 1963:   Join S/m *Token*
February 1964:   Leave *Token* for hospital
March 1964:   Join S/m *Rorqual*
July 1964:   Leave *Rorqual*
July1964:   Join S/m *Porpoise*
Dec 1964:   Leave *Porpoise*/ Draft to Royal Naval Barracks Portsmouth for Re Hab. course
                         Recalled to Dolphin for draft to un-named S/m
                         Draft to un-named S/m cancelled
Dec 1964   Leave service

71

It was a total of eight different submarines served; add two extra for *Turpin* and one for *Trump,* plus two drafts cancelled and one changed. I probably hold a few records. I certainly know of no one who had more drafts or served on more submarines, even among those who served a lot longer.

Years of Cold War patrols 'unrecognised'

I NOTED with interest that the MOD had recently authorised the peacekeeping bar "Air Cover Gulf" for award with the 1962 General Service Medal.

As an ex-submariner it would appear that the Royal Navy's Submarine Branch has been omitted from such recognition, despite being at the forefront of our country's deterrent and making a major contribution to post war world stability.

I am of course referring to the unique role of both the conventional and nuclear submarines during that period in our history known as the Cold War.

Our qualifying period was not just a mere 30 days, but years of arduous patrols and covert operations in the pursuit of world peace.

Yet to this day we still remain unrecognised.

As a professional, highly sustained elite branch of the Royal Navy, it is my opinion that recognition should still be given, in the form of a 'Cold War' bar to the 1962 GSM, especially during this our centenary year.

That recognition would go a long way to eliminating the pride, high level of morale and esprit de corps that still exists within the ranks of the Submarine Association. – N. R. Simpson, ex-Barton (SM), Hull.

Cold war article

Copy of newspaper article

Submarines *Aeneas* (left) and *Turpin* (right) alongside at Dolphin.

Note the square shape of the ballast tanks of the 'A'
boat and the round tanks of the 'T' boat.

Submarine *Turpin*

Submarine *Ambush*

Note the height of the bridge on the *Ambush* compared to that of the *Turpin*.

Submarines *Andrew*, *Ambush*, and *Amphion* alongside depot ship HMS *Medway*, part of 7th Submarine Squadron based at Singapore.

Submarine *Token*. Basic 'T' Class, not converted to Super 'T'

H.M.S. "PORPOISE"

Submarine *Porpoise*. The first of the 'P' Class.
Another of the diesel electric type.

The last of the diesel electric submarines to be built
were the 'O' Class, similar to the 'P' Class.

CIVVY STREET

On the first day of my demob leave I went to see what I think was called the rehabilitation officer in Birmingham, who suggested that as it was so near Christmas it was no good looking for a permanent job. However, he said that I should try the Post Office, as at this time of year they took on a lot of temporary staff to cover the extra workload. He made the appointment and I got a job until Christmas sorting parcels. I decided during this time to ask for a permanent job, as I learnt from other employees that good money could be earned with all of the overtime available. I was accepted and did a short course and was then employed once again in the parcels department awaiting a driving examination before being transferred to driving.

It was a shift system, six till two, two till ten, and ten till six, and each week I would put my name on the overtime register. If I was on afternoons, I would ask for a night shift as overtime; on nights I would ask for an afternoon shift. On mornings I tried not to have any, giving me my afternoons free, but it didn't always work out, as I would be allocated an afternoon shift if there was no one else to cover it. When I complained, I was told it was all or nothing, so if I refused I wouldn't get any overtime at all. So although the money was good, I felt that I wasn't really living, with working sixteen hours a day six days a week, with occasionally a week of afternoons off, so I started looking for something else.

I eventually found what I was looking for in wiring control panels. I stayed at one company for about a year, then moved to another where I soon became a charge hand. I was asked to carry out modifications to some control panels that the company had built, then installed at Cowley for the new Maxi production line. I picked up Baz on the way one very cold winter Sunday morning about 6 a.m, to enable us to get a full day's work in on site. The job took us most of the day, and the MD turned up late afternoon to see how things had progressed; after testing, we eventually left at about six in the evening. We hadn't stopped all day and hadn't eaten or had a drink, as there were no facilities open on a Sunday. On approaching Shipston on Stour, there were a couple of nasty bends, and we ended up in a ditch upside down with three of the four doors wedged shut. We managed to escape through the one opening door to find that a car had stopped to help and that the driver had injured himself when he slipped on the icy road. He gave us a lift into Shipston where we phoned one of the family to come and pick us up. We also rang the police and had to visit them the following day. They also commented on the state of the road, but I think the accident was mainly due to tiredness. I was without transport for a while, and the management allowed me to use the company van until Mrs A. found out. Then it was back to the bus for a while.

Shortly afterwards, I was made foreman, and finally production manager within a space of about two years. During my rise, I got on really well with the managing director, who seemed impressed with my capabilities and offered me a contract to do the site installations and commissioning of the control panels that we were building for the new Birmingham Post Office. The conditions were such that I could only carry out the work outside of normal working hours, so that it did not interfere with my in house day job. This also included any of the other workforces that I employed. After a few weeks of working evenings and weekends, he asked if I would also take on another contract for the new Manchester Post Office. This I did and increased the workforce, working evenings at Birmingham and weekends at Manchester.

When I first started with this company, we used to have a scrap metal merchant visit every couple of weeks to take the scrap wire, and he would take about two hundred weight and pay the foreman two pounds, who, in agreement with the management, would put it in a kitty to be shared among the workers at Christmas. When I took the job as foreman, I decided that we could make more money if we took the scrap ourselves and burnt off the insulation and sold it directly to the scrap yard. This I did with the help of a young lad named Baz; we did it successfully, and a much bigger bonus was distributed at Christmas, something like an extra week's pay as opposed to the two pounds previously—to the delight of all the of workers.

Although I got on with the MD, it was a different story with his wife, who ran the office, and her favourite, the buyer, who was a previous production manager. We had many altercations, and I think it is fair to say that she disliked me and my methods, even though I was making more money for her company. When I took over as production manager, the turnover was about eight thousand pounds per month, and each month it increased. Previously it was restricted by man power and their unwillingness to work extra for an ungrateful management, as previous foremen and production managers had not been concerned with the interests of the workers. As I had been one of them, I wanted to change this, and the Christmas bonus showed them that I was on their side.

I suggested that apart from the one self-employed outworker that we had, we should allow our own workforce to be able to take work home and be paid a price for each job. It was agreed, and this helped with output; then I learned that the self-employed outworker was being paid more for the same work, and I confronted the MD's wife. Her answer was that he had greater overheads. I couldn't believe that a woman who claimed to be a good business woman could make that statement, and, in the ensuing argument, the MD came out of his office and asked what the hell all the noise was about. She got in first with her argument, but fortunately the MD agreed with me, and the lads got paid the extra for their outwork.

My next confrontation was with the buyer; although production was increasing, he didn't seem to be allowing for it. At one time work was brought to a standstill when we ran out of cable markers, and I went to see him about it. His answer was, "I ordered the same number that we usually have." "But if production is increasing," I said, "Surely it's obvious that we need more." Mrs A. got involved, and another heated argument ensued until the MD once again intervened and told him to get in his car and fetch some so that the men could continue with their work.

Shortly afterwards, the company moved to larger premises to cope with the extra workload. The monthly turnover was now around thirty thousand, and another tier of management was brought in who took the side of Mrs A. They fought against the idea that the MD had suggested, to set me up as a subsidiary of the company, with some of the existing workers in a different factory leaving more room for expansion.

I gathered from Mrs A.'s attitude towards me that she would get rid of me if the opportunity arose, and someone unintentionally handed her that opportunity on a plate. One of the lads whom I didn't particularly like had apparently stolen some rolls of heavy cable, cut it up, and stripped it of its insulation. He was caught red-handed by the police at the scrap merchants. His excuse was that I had sent him there with scrap. I knew nothing of this until I was sent for by Mrs A., who had two detectives with her. I gave my side of the story and produced my accounts of the Christmas bonus kitty. Mrs A. denied knowledge of any agreement regarding the Christmas bonus, although I offered the telephone number of the foreman whom I had originally relieved as witness as well as a former production manager. They were never contacted. I could see that I was on a hiding to nothing and said "Well you've been looking for an excuse to get rid of me, so don't bother. I resign." She said, "Hand over the kitty, and I won't press charges." I looked at the detectives for a comment but got none, so I walked away. I did go to see a solicitor who said that I had a case, but it could be long and costly and he advised me to forget it. I didn't get what was owed to me on my outside contracts either. I did, however, have the last laugh—as the company went bankrupt about six months later.

Whilst working there, a couple of the lads showed an interest in submarines, so I offered to take them to Gosport and show them around. We set off early one Saturday morning and eventually arrived at the main gate of HMS *Dolphin* where I had a chat with the two guys manning the gate. This was before the days of high security, and they let us in. We walked down to the jetty, and to my surprise found that the *Ambush* was alongside, outboard of the *Opossum*. The sentry on the *Opossum* was a guy whom I knew, and he said that he would finish his watch shortly and invited us below when we had finished on the *Ambush*. He spoke to the sentry on the *Ambush* to verify that I was who I said I was, and we went below. Whilst showing the lads around, I met another couple of crew members whom I had known. Before we had finished the tour, we were confronted by the duty officer whom I didn't know, and he was none too pleased. He called for the trot sentry and gave him an earful, and the trot sentry explained that my ID had been verified. However, he still wasn't happy. I did explain that I had spent 2.5 years trying to get off this boat, and now he was saying that I wasn't allowed on it. Then the sentry was told to not let us off the boat until he returned, which suited me as we could now finish the tour. He apparently reported the situation to Commander S/M and also reported the two main gate sentries for allowing us in. The Commander's attitude was completely different, and he suggested that as my ID had been verified, no charges should be brought against anyone and that we should be treated as welcome guests. We then said our goodbyes to the *Ambush* duty watch and joined Sid on the *Opossum*, and he had plenty of rum to spare. We spent most of the afternoon on board and finally staggered back to the main gate. My guests had thoroughly enjoyed their visit and talked of nothing else for the next few days.

A NEW BEGINNING

By the time I heard of the company's bankruptcy, I'd started up with Baz as my partner carrying out electrical contracts, and wiring factories and houses, as well as building control panels. For the most part, we kept busy and were doing quite well. Most of our work was local, and we bought an ex GPO van from an auction that served us well.

During our travels around the Midlands, we were listening to a news flash on the radio about a multi pile up on the motorway in fog, just as we passed a factory with a sign in the driveway that said, "Speed Bumps," (large tarmac mounds across the road). Which prompted me to comment; that it was a pity they didn't have portable speed bumps for such occasions as that which we were listening to. This started a debate on the possibilities, and we started visiting rubber and plastic moulding companies to see if anyone could help in the construction of a portable ramp. However, we didn't get any joy. When Baz got home that night, he rang me to say, "Could we not get mouldings made like large flat pudding basins?" We discussed this the following day, and I remembered that we had worked recently for the managing director of a road asphalting company. I decided that we should seek his advice or that of his contacts. He tried to help us, but got nowhere—only that it would cost a fortune for a prototype. So the idea was shelved until I decided that we could actually make one.

Back to a rubber company to buy some sheets of rubber about 0.75 inch thick, cut out a disc about 18 inches in diameter and cut the centre out of this, cut another smaller disc the same shape slightly larger than the one cut out of the first, stick it onto the first disc covering the cut out, and finally a small, solid disc to cover the remaining aperture—and we had our first prototype. It was very heavy and cumbersome, but the principal was there. We built four of these and approached our asphalt man again, who had just finished a road that was not yet open to the public. Off we went to test them with great success. He was so impressed that he offered to financially back us—which we had to accept, as we were fast running out of funds. We had already had a meeting with a patent solicitor and learnt that the cost of patenting was about a thousand pounds per country, and funding further development would have been difficult without outside help. We eventually took patents out in seventeen countries.

I wrote to the Road Research Laboratories explaining the principal, and their reply was that it was not feasible as they had already tried putting numerous objects in the road. As vehicles drove over them, the objects were picked up and strewn across the highway. I also rang BBC Midlands Today and briefly explained what we had. I was told yes, they would be interested—and they asked if I could take one in that afternoon. I was introduced to the then-presenter Tom Coyne, and I explained its function; it was exhibited on that evening's program. About a week later, I had a phone call from a Robert Symes Schutzman, asking if we could let him have samples for his team to assess for a possible feature on *Tomorrow's World*. We delivered them to the studios in London, where we met presenters Mike Rod, Raymond Baxter, James Burke, and the producer Robert Symes Schutzman.

After a chat and a chance meeting with Patrick Moore, we left our samples with them for evaluation.

During this time, we won a contract with a company who had built a conveyer track system for Thorn. The job was in Gateshead, where they manufactured their radiators, and our contract was to design and install the electrics to the system. We decided to travel by car as we didn't think the van was up to such a journey; we left home in the early hours of the morning to enable us to get a day's work in once on site. We spent the first day designing and ordering the materials from the local wholesaler, to be delivered first thing the following morning. We paid cash, as we didn't have an account. By this time, it was late evening and we found a hotel named The Springfield to be quite convenient to the site.

The following morning after breakfast, we discovered that the car had been stolen from the hotel car park. The manager called the police and details were taken.

Without tools, we would have great difficulty completing the work at all, let alone within the time frame given. We reported our problem to the management on site, who said that we could use their labour with their tools to help us. The materials that we had ordered were duly delivered, and we started organizing the installation. As it happened, the workers were reluctant to let us use their tools and, understandably, they wouldn't allow us to use them without them being there, which included all of their rather long tea and lunch breaks, and at four thirty they packed up and went home. I didn't hold this against them, as I didn't think it was fair for the management to expect them to work under these conditions. I couldn't find any management to complain to, so left it until the following morning, by which time they had gotten wind of the fact that we were not very happy and called a meeting in one of their offices. I pointed out our problems and said that I would prefer that they find someone else to do the job. I was prepared to stay and explain what needed doing, but trying to work ourselves under the existing arrangements seemed impossible. One of the management left the office and came back about five minutes later and said, "I've just spoken to your boss, and we've agreed that you two have got to split up and take on our labour working twelve-hour day and night shifts." I could just imagine working a twelve-hour night shift with their already disgruntled workforce. I asked him whom he had spoken to—Mr Harris or Mr Ward? "Mr Ward," he said. "That's strange," I said. "That's Barry Ward," pointing at Baz, "and I'm Rick Harris, and there is no one else, and we're now going home." We left, walked back to the hotel, checked out, and travelled home by train, leaving all of the materials that we had paid for on site. The frustrating part was that if we'd travelled up by van, we would have been insured, but we weren't covered in the car for loss of tools, etc. The van probably wouldn't have been stolen either.

Shortly afterwards, we had a message from the BBC saying that the tests they had carried out were successful and that could we arrange to pick up the discs, refurbish and tart them up, and await further instructions. We took them to where we had our control panels painted and had them coloured day glow orange.

Meanwhile, I had a telephone call from the police in Newcastle, who had recovered my car, wanting to know if I could make arrangements to pick it up.

Baz and I travelled up again by train and met with the police. The boot had been forced open and all of the tools, as well as the radio, were gone, but at least the car was driveable. We were then asked to look through some recovered items to see if any of them belonged to, us but only the megger was ours.

So we needed to buy two new complete sets of tools. In conversation with the police, we were informed that they had caught the guy responsible, and I mentioned what I would like to do to him. The officer then surprised me by saying, "Would you like his address?" I thought it was too good to be true: "Durham prison, and you'll have a long wait if you still want to meet him." Apparently, he was caught assaulting another victim during a theft, and then seriously injured the police officer who tried to restrain him. He was being charged with two counts of GBH and would be spending some time behind bars, and when the courts were finished with him, the army wanted him for something similar as well as for desertion. So the officer's advice was for me to put it behind me and get on with my life.

It was the following week when we were asked to meet the producer of *Tomorrow's World* at his house in Guildford at seven in the morning, complete with discs, to make the film for the *Tomorrow's World* program. This meant an early start for us, since we had to drive there. We had breakfast with him, and the rest of the team started to arrive at about eight thirty. He had told us the time of seven because he knew that we had a distance to travel and worried that we may be late and cock up the schedule; as it was, we were about half an hour early. During our wait, he showed us around his house, garden, and miniature railway; he was apparently an enthusiast. Around nine o'clock, we set off for the film site, which was where the Harrier Jump Jet was being tested. I think it was at Vickers, and a perimeter road had been hired for the day, along with all sorts of vehicles from a vintage car to an articulated lorry; even the police were in attendance with scene of accident equipment. My role was to drive a breakdown lorry. During the morning, a film was made of a mock up accident in which the police were in attendance without the discs and trying to warn the oncoming traffic to slow down, with Mike Rod driving the vintage car with his arm round a girl, not paying attention to the road, and the rest of us following in various other vehicles. Filming had to be suspended on occasions when they wound up the Harriers, as the noise drowned everything else. We were all taken to lunch in small groups to different venues by Vickers public relations officers. I ended up with, among others, Mike Rod and his girlfriend for the day. She, coincidently, happened to be the producer's daughter, Roberta. (Maybe he wanted a son.)

The afternoon was a repeat of the morning, with the inclusion of the discs in order to show what a difference could be made. It was wonderful free advertising, and for the next few days we were inundated with phone calls for information with more enquiries in the post. A lot of the enquiries were for factory sites, hospitals, power stations, and the like, which made us think that we needed two types—as the originals were designed for traffic travelling at speeds of 70 mph, and these people wanted to slow their traffic to 5–10 mph. We wrote to all of them explaining the situation and informed them that we would send them details once we had the modified item in production.

We did, however, have numerous enquiries from police forces who wanted us to demonstrate the product to them. One of the first places that we visited was the Home Office Scientific Department at Harpenden. The people whom we met were mainly high-ranking police officers involved in traffic policing. They were impressed, but said that they would take up too much room in a police vehicle, as did traffic cones. I answered that these were only the prototypes and that the finished articles would be stackable like large dinner plates and linked together with a pair of rubber ties. We anticipated linking nine of them together, and that stack would measure about 15inches high by 18 inches wide, and the ties would act as handles for carrying them when they were stacked. If they were placed on the hard shoulder in a stack and run across the carriageway while holding the handle of the top disc, the rest would follow and would cover a distance of 27 feet laid out. They were very keen and suggested that we contact them again when we had the finished article. Jokingly, I said, "And by that time, we will have redesigned the cones for you." "I look forward to seeing that too," one said.

Within the next few days, the first few samples were coming off the press and my thoughts had moved to redesigning the traffic cone. We visited a spring manufacturing company and asked them to make a couple of samples of what I had drawn, a conical shaped bed spring about eighteen inches high, eight inches at the base and tapering to one inch at the top. We fed over the wire spring a day glow orange sleeve. We then attached the spring to a hollow plastic base that we had vacuum formed, which could be filled with water or sand for stability. We had gleaned from the traffic police that one of the problems with the normal cone was that it was not stable in winds over 45 mph, and on many occasions a lorry passing could create enough draught to blow it over. We had also formed a small cone for the top of the spring. Pushing down on the top would cause the whole spring to depress into a cavity in the base, thus taking up less space for storage.

We took our prototypes along with two normal cones to the wind tunnel at MIRA for testing. The two standard cones took off in wind speeds between 45 and 50 mph, but our prototypes, apart from being more visible because of their movement, were still standing at 75 mph. The testing was deemed a success.

Meanwhile, we were now visiting and demonstrating to police forces all over the country the 'Hazard Warning Discs.' Their only concern was that they couldn't really use them without informing the public what they were all about. We'd had a contact name given to us at the DOE (Department of the Environment) and had written to him but had not received a reply, so whilst in London we decided to call on him. We then learnt why we hadn't had a reply; the man had been on holiday and was ill on returning and was now on sick leave, so we asked if we could see someone else. We could hear him coming along the corridor saying, "No, no we're not interested; if they can't go through the proper channels, they'll get nowhere with me."

He did see us, however, and was not very pleasant. We learnt later that we had approached the head of department direct and that his underling was not pleased about it.

We revisited the Home Office Scientific Department with the genuine articles and offered to supply a set for free, thinking of the further orders that these people could generate for us, but they insisted on paying. Therefore, we walked away with our first order and promised to return with the production version of the cone, the prototype of which they liked very much.

Our next order came from Birmingham Council, who used them on the Aston Expressway with the press in attendance, so we had more free publicity via ITV, BBC, and some newspapers. Then we heard from the council that they were not allowed to use them, as they were illegal.

Meanwhile, we had made arrangements with the RRL (Road Research Laboratories) to demonstrate them to the police, and we also invited the DOE.

Our team consisted of myself, Baz, our backer, and the MD and tool designer from our manufacturers. The police had the most people, about thirty high-ranking officers. There were six from the Laboratories, two from the DOE, the top man and his deputy of whom we had already fallen foul, and representatives from the AA and RAC. Also laid on by the Lab people were two motor cyclists and a couple of cars. The weather was foul, pouring with rain, and we all congregated on what was like an airport runway at the RRL.

We laid out two sets of discs, and the cars and motor cycles ran over them numerous times, increasing speed each time. The drivers were then asked for their comments, and all were favourable. I then noticed one of the staff from the RRL lifting one of the discs, so I went over to him and asked what he was looking for. He wanted to know what we had used to stick them to the road, as he had been the author of the letter stating that it was impossible to achieve what we had just achieved. The answer was that because of their shape, they behaved like suckers, and in the weather that we were experiencing right then, they worked extremely well.

Back at the conference, our deputy from the DOE was still not convinced, despite a heated debate from a number of the police explaining that this was what they needed. DOE was saying that they were illegal, and one of the police officers was asking why.

"Because they are over three quarters of an inch high."

"But we put many things in the road that are higher, such as the traffic cones."

"We have a law allowing us to use those."

"Well give us a law allowing us to use these."

""What do you want us to do?"

"We can't just start using them; we need to advise the public of our intention to use them."

"It's a propriety item, and you want us to spend money advertising them so that these people can make a fortune? No way."

"They could save lives."

"Use them and prove them, then we'll talk again."

"How can we? You tell us that we will be breaking the law and, as we said, we daren't use them without informing the public first."

We left there wet and depressed, and to make matters worse, within the next week we had two visitors, one from South Africa and one from Germany. Both wanted to know where they could see them being used with the view to import them to their countries. We had to tell them the situation, and they promptly lost interest.

We still had the industrial version to work on in addition to the traffic cone, but our problem now, after paying for the patents and the tooling, was finance. Our backer was prepared to fund the tooling for the industrial version, but a quote for the plastic spring alone was nearly twenty thousand pounds in addition to the base—so now we were looking at a total investment of around £50,000, which is a lot of money even now, let alone in 1972.

Through the tool maker, we were put in touch with someone from Lucas and we arranged a meeting. At that time, apparently they were looking to get into this market. With subsequent meetings that involved more of the Lucas hierarchy, they decided they would like to take on all three items, which meant that they would pay for the tooling for the cone. We were negotiating for royalties, hoping for an offer at the next meeting. Then the meeting was cancelled, and later that day we heard on the news that Lucas were in financial difficulties with lots of workers being made redundant. We tried to contact them for information, but no one was ever available. So twice now we felt like we had won the lottery but lost the ticket. We did manage to get the industrial version off the ground, and I decided to get back to building control panels to help out with the finances whilst Baz concentrated on the speed bumps. We had taken on his wife temporarily, as she was out of work and we needed someone, but as far as I was concerned she was a disaster. She would not cooperate with me in my side of the business, and life once again became very difficult, in addition to the strain of going through a divorce from my wife Pat at the time.

I won a contract with a company that I had been dealing with for a few years, to build three large control panels. Once we had delivered them and the invoice had been presented, Baz's wife took it upon herself to demand payment after a week, no doubt to impress our backer. Normally I would have left it a couple of weeks and then spoken to my contact at the company and gotten him use his influence to get us early payment, rather than wait for the usual thirty or sixty days. But on this occasion, she must have upset someone who then upset her, and she then reported this to our backer. He, not being given all the facts, contacted the company and threatened to sue if we weren't paid forthwith. All of this went on without my knowledge; when I found out, I went to see our backer to let him know that the next contract would have been worth in the region of ten thousand pounds, but that because of what had happened, we would not get any more work from them. I explained that I was not happy with the situation, with me having been undermined, and suggested that we replace Baz's wife. He wouldn't hear of it, so I suggested that they buy me out, which he agreed to. As the patents were all in the name of the company, I had no rights to them. He suggested a figure, which was not as much as I would have liked. However, as he said at the time, he could shut the company down and start again without me, and that wouldn't cost as much as I was being offered. So I accepted and, not for the first time, I would start again from scratch.

The Birmingham Post, Friday, September 29, 1972 _____ MIDLAND NEWS 9

'Bumpies' to make drivers sit up

Birmingham Post Reporter

Portable rubber "bumps" to give advance warning of road hazards were described as a real contribution to road safety after a demonstration on one lane of the Aston Expressway yesterday.

Birmingham has bought the first six sets of "bumpies" designed and produced by a newly-formed company at Northfield, Birmingham, and plans to use them on the Expressway and Queensway.

Coun. William Sowton, chairman of Birmingham Public Works Committee, said after the demonstration: "Having driven over them, I am quite certain they are going to make an impact on people. I think they are a very good idea and will be a real contribution to safety.

The city's observations on the bumps will be passed on to the Home Office, which is assessing the advantages of recommending their use by police forces.

SOMETHING WENT BUMP . . . and a driver who has missed seeing a warning notice is made aware that a hazard lies ahead. Birmingham Public Works Department has bought the first four sets of hazard warning discs made by Hazard Warning Systems Ltd., of Northfield, Birmingham. Above (left) police and Public Works Department officers watch a test of the discs on Aston Expressway yesterday. Above (right) two sets of the 2½-inch-high discs are strung across a lane ahead of a diversion.

Newspaper cutting. Portable speed bumps, first used on the Aston Expressway leading to Spaghetti Junction.

Testing site on perimeter road of Birmingham Airport.

Cross-sectional view of Hazard Warning disc
showing stacking arrangement.

Prototype of cones

Showing stacking arrangement of cones

START AGAIN

I spoke to my contact at the company for which we had built the control panels and apologised for all of the hassle that had been caused. He said that he would offer me more work but that I would not be able to use the name of Harris in the new company heading. I decided to register the new company name of 'Richard Dice,' DICE being short for Domestic, Industrial, and Commercial Electrics.

I also approached other people whom I'd gotten to know in the Hockley Centre where we had our premises as Hazard Warning Systems Ltd. It was in the new jewellery quarter. It also coincided with the Hockley Centre being extended, so I was inundated with work.

The first new unit that I worked in was for John, a jeweller whom I'd known for some time and who was expanding into casting his own designs. He had employed a guy, Ron, to set up and run the casting side of the business. I had quoted for the electrics, and near completion John called in to see how things were going. I explained that I'd allowed for the electrics to be continued along an internal wall yet to be built. He suggested that I should not only build it but also do the plumbing and build a mezzanine floor. I was not very experienced at these things, but I agreed to do it. I managed the wall and also the plumbing, but I called in the help of a couple of friends of mine, Brian and Roger of Unispray Ltd. (Brian was to be my best man at my second wedding.) They would build the extra floor, as they dealt in steelwork as well as many other things including plumbing. I had turned to these guys for advice on the plumbing. We also did all of the painting and decorating.

Whilst working in the area some time later, I called in to see Ron, with whom I'd gotten on very well. He told me that he was parting company with John and taking on a new unit, and that could I do the same for him as I had for John. This I did gladly.

As work was still coming in, I decided to take on some help and employed a neighbour, Malcolm, who had just left school. He was a tall, thin, blond-haired, gangly lad, but very pleasant. He was into music in a big way, and his ambition was to become a rock star; he was already in a group. On one occasion, we were working at a factory full of girls in West Bromwich, and the previous night he had performed at Barbarellas in Birmingham and had had his hair coloured purple . He had been told that it would wash out completely, but when he turned up for work that morning he looked like a live match with his bright pink hair. Some of the girls had been winding him up, and a rather large one came up to him, grabbed him, and asked, "Am yo is or am yo aint a punk rocka?" He suffered on every site that we visited, but he took it well.

We often worked alongside Brian and Roger, as they had taken on maintenance contracts for a group of car component manufacturers, and they used us for the electrical side. We had free use of the company's equipment to help in our work, including forklift trucks to move machinery around when re-siting, etc. On one occasion, the men went on strike because in the one area it was too cold. We were asked by management to take one of the lorries over to another of their factories and pick up one of their large oil-fired blower heaters and install it in the cold area. We returned with the said heater and I commandeered a fork lift truck. Just as I had the forks under it, the union rep took the keys out of the ignition. I was now not allowed to drive the truck. I argued that they were on strike because they were cold, and that I was about to rectify that. He was not interested, and it took three hours of negotiation between union and management before one of their lads took the heater off the lorry and positioned it for us to install. My other brush with their union was at mealtime. We normally had lunch in their canteen after they had had theirs, as agreed. We had just sat down with our meal when this same union man told us to leave, as he had called a meeting, so we had to take our meal outside even though it was snowing at the time. After the meeting, a lot of the lads came to us and apologized for this man's behaviour, and the following day he was ousted on a vote of no confidence. Justice!

Another time, for some reason, I was helping Roger on a plumbing job in a new building. The first fix of electrics had been installed, and some electricians came to carry out the second fix. The man in charge kept going from one set of cables to another, and after a while said to his lads, "I can't sort this out; we'll have to go back and find out who did the first fix." Being inquisitive, I had already looked at the wiring and sorted out the coding. I offered to show him, and he was most grateful that a 'plumber' could solve his problem for him. We also worked at Shotton steel works for a few weeks, helping to fit the pipework that they had manufactured for what was known as the colour coat line.

My most memorable occasion working with Brian was when we were erecting an internal screen between the loading area and the packing area at BSR on the Waterfall Trading Estate, a job that entailed a lot of welding. Brian was not very keen on heights, and I had built a scaffold tower to reach the apex where we were to start welding struts to the existing roof. It took many cups of tea before I could get him out of the canteen and up the tower. We finally got started and worked for the rest of the day, arranging to meet on site the following morning. As I entered the estate, I was passed by a fire engine just leaving and didn't give it a second thought until I saw Brian sitting in his car away from the building, and another fire engine at the building where we should be working. I parked alongside him and he got into my car. He said he couldn't go in alone, as he needed moral support in case the fire was anything that he had caused. We learnt on entering the building that it was. Apparently whilst welding, some of the sparks had fallen out of sight into the roof space and had smouldered all night, and when the door was opened first thing that morning, the inrush of air set the whole lot ablaze. A lot of damage was done, and he spent the rest of the day talking to the management, the fire service, and his insurance company.

Malcolm and I had been working in some terrible conditions on a building site in ice and snow; the temperature was around zero, and we were taking turns climbing the ladder to the top of each telegraph pole to make the electrical connections to the various site huts. I thought that my hands were bad in the cold, but Malcolm suffered worse. I think from then on he decided that this life was not for him, so when I loaned him to one of my clients whilst I was on holiday, he was asked if he would like to work for them full time and he accepted. I think he made the right decision, as he ended up running the business a few years later and became very wealthy. The company was involved in copper, silver, and gold etching. I had first worked for them in the Hockley Centre, and then set up their machinery in their new premises. This had been around the time when Charles and Diana were getting married, as I remember that they made thousands of commemorative plates in gold and silver. At the end of each working day, they paid me to take a car load to a factory in Coventry for finishing and bring back the previous days load.

If anyone had known what I was carrying at the time, I would have been a good target for a highjack. I think the value of each load was in the region of fifty thousand pounds.

I had also done a lot of work for another control panel company, Floorplan. Sometimes panels would be required on site before they could be completed, and due to unavailability of components, I would be asked to go to the site to complete the work and to commission them. I had a phone call from their MD asking me to attend a site with him, with the view to me taking on the commissioning of all of the controls at a new build site. It was an animal research laboratory somewhere in Hertfordshire, and would take about four months to complete. We agreed on a price for a daily rate, travel, and accommodation, and work started the following week towards the end of January. After being on site for a couple of weeks, I came home for the weekend and we had a heavy snow fall. I went with Barbara, my then wife, and a few of our friends to the Lickey Hills with our sledges for the Sunday afternoon. On the last run of the day, Barbara and her sister were on one of the larger sledges, and someone gave them a push for good measure. Unfortunately, they were sitting rather than lying, and as they dug their feet in, they were blinded by the snow spray and didn't see the tree for which they were headed. They hit the tree at some speed; Margaret, at the rear, was okay, but Barbara took the full force with a leg on either side of the tree. Someone ran to a local house and called an ambulance, and I realised when she couldn't move that some damage must have been done. I was reluctant to move her, but it was bitterly cold. It was getting dark and we were at the bottom of a rather steep hill. I decided that the best thing to do was to get her to lay back where she was on the sledge, and we would pull her back to the top of the hill. One of the local residents suggested that we carry her into his house on the sledge until the ambulance arrived. When it arrived, we were rushed off to Bromsgrove Hospital where an X-ray showed that she had broken her pelvis in addition to the injury done to her badly bruised face and chest. She was obviously confined to her hospital bed, and I had the job of taking her younger sister to her parents' house and breaking the news. It was suggested that she be moved to another hospital, but as we had a doctor friend working in the hospital where she was, I asked if she could stay there.

I obviously couldn't continue with my contract; fortunately, I was put in touch with an engineer living in Manchester who had just returned from working in Saudi Arabia. I took him to the site, and he offered to do the work for half of the price I was being paid. Which meant that I could employ him on a sub contract basis. I would visit the site once a week for a meeting and pick up his report, and it worked very well. He was probably better qualified to do the job than I was; his only problem was he was too helpful in so much that he would carry out tasks that we were not paid to do. I pointed this out to him, but he continued; I then had to explain to him that if he did it again, I would not pay for anything that we were not contracted to do. He would then have to negotiate with the main contractor for payment for any extra work, as I had to justify my bill to the company that I was invoicing—hence the reports.

Towards the end of the contract, I was offered another contract with the same company on a different site. Shortly afterwards, the MD found out how much I was paying this other guy and decided to give the contract to him. I did point out to him that I thought I had earned my money, as I had visited the site each week and also had a meeting with the MD at his office to go through the report each week, and generally liaised with the site management. Also if no one controlled this guy, he would cost them dearly—but my pleas fell on deaf ears.

About two months later, I heard via the grapevine that the company had gone out of business, mainly because this guy, as their representative, had signed documents taking on a larger part of the new contract that was not financially viable.

I visited my wife each evening, and after two weeks I was told that I could have her at home as long as I could look after her full time. She would need to spend the next ten weeks flat on her back. She would also need to return to the hospital each week for a blood test, as she had developed a DVT, was taking Warfarin, and needed to be closely monitored. This was the time of the NUPE strikes, so I couldn't have an ambulance to take her home. I had to borrow a stretcher from the St John's Ambulance, and with the help of my friend and his camper van, we had to do all of the lifting and carrying from her bed to our home. Our doctor, who lived directly across the road from us, was waiting to greet us. He was horrified when he watched the next episode. The front door opened directly onto the stairs, which led to a small landing at the top, and our bedroom was immediately on the right. There was not enough room to negotiate the turn with the stretcher flat, and my instructions were to not let her put any weight on her legs under any circumstances. Therefore, we tied her into the stretcher and carried her up feet first, stood her on her head at the top of the stairs, and lowered her into the bedroom, singeing her nose on the radiator in the process. The doctor said there was no way that we could go through this every week, and he agreed to come in each week take the blood, after which I would take it to the hospital. He also arranged for a nurse to visit.

A week or so before the total of twelve weeks of lying flat was completed, she started developing pains in her stomach. During the night, I called the doctor, who turned out to be a locum and didn't seem duly concerned. The following day, she hadn't improved, and I called the doctor again, It was our own doctor on this occasion, who examined her and called for an ambulance. She was taken to Dudley Road Hospital. Once she was there, since she had been admitted with a stomach complaint, they tried to get her to walk, and she had great difficulty convincing them that her stomach wasn't the only problem. The doctor who examined her said that it was probably the fact that she had been lying still for so long that resulted in her digestive system not correctly eliminating. Once this was sorted out, she started to feel well and was soon able to walk again. Since she had improved so much, we couldn't understand why she wasn't allowed home. As no one would give us a reason, she was ready to discharge herself. I was a little concerned, so I invited our female doctor friend to visit with me. At first, she was also baffled, so went to see the ward sister, introduced herself and got an explanation. When she returned, she strongly advised Barbara to not discharge herself, as she may have a stroke. Apparently, somewhere along the line someone had overdosed her, and her blood was now too thin. Therefore, this needed time to right itself before she would be safe. A week or so later, she was back home and once had regained her strength. Then life got back to its normal, hectic pace again.

I had an enquiry from someone whom I had briefly met who was involved in reclamation; his company would be called in after a fire or flood to salvage what it could of the equipment or machinery and to get things working again as much as possible. He asked if I would be prepared to work in Oman for a while, to which I agreed.

I was about to go on holiday to tour France with Barbara when the enquiry came in, and the guy, Vic, said that no date had been set to start, so we should go ahead with our plans and ring him each day for further news. Once we got as far as Brittany, I decide to go no farther, and we spent two weeks there before I got a flight date of three days hence. We then headed home and just had time to sort things out before meeting the rest of the team at Birmingham airport—except for Vic, who had gone ahead to sort out accommodation and contacts.

I was one of two electricians in the team, along with Vic and three others who would strip and rebuild the machinery/plant in a dairy, which had been flooded not far from the capital Muscat. We flew to Heathrow for our connecting flight, which was a 747 to Muscat; we were the only passengers in Club Class. We had left Birmingham on Saturday afternoon, and arrived in Oman at about mid day local time Sunday. We were booked into the Intercontinental Hotel and we picked up two hire cars and, as Sunday is a normal working day, Vic and I went off to meet some of the contacts for rewinding motors and obtaining electrical spares. From then on, our working day was from six in the morning until four in the afternoon, six days a week.

It was June, and the temperature was a searing 130 F. The pool and sea temperature was 112 F, and getting from one's sun lounger to the pool without shoes was quite painful. There were signs on the beach warning of severe burns from the red hot sand even first thing in the morning The hotel was air conditioned to 85 F, and each morning before six when we opened the door of the hotel, it was like opening the door to an oven, as the outside temperature was already over 100 F. I always took a couple of apples from breakfast to eat later in the day. One time I left them in the car, as I was going to drive to Muscat at eight o'clock to pick up some spares. By this time, the apples were well and truly baked.

For the first few days, we would get back to the hotel, get a drink, and spend a couple of hours by the pool before going in for our meal; however, things changed when Ramadan started. The law was very strict, and we were warned of the consequences if we were caught breaking it: "No eating drinking or smoking during daylight hours." We could still go for a swim, but to have a drink, even tea, we had to go into a small room out of sight. This applied to all of the daylight hours, which made life rather difficult for us, as up until this time we were calling in on our way to site to pick up two or three litres of water each. We drank these during the days work, and even then we only went for a pee once a day, and that came out like treacle. But to have a drink of water now meant going to a room set aside for us.

The ban on smoking would not normally have bothered me, but the rest of the crew were smokers and would smoke in the car. We had been warned of the police looking out for this, known as the tobacco patrols, and since I was one of the drivers, I would have been thrown into prison with them if caught. This came very close to happening on one occasion, and after that I refused to drive them or even get in the car with them if they smoked.

Apparently, it rarely rains in this part of Oman, but a few weeks earlier it had rained, and all of the water came down from the mountains. The infrastructure was not designed to cope with so much water, so the dairy where we were working had been flooded to a depth of four feet six inches. It was in quite a mess; the layer of mud had been partly cleared away, but all of the machinery and equipment affected was still caked with mud. Our job was to strip the entire plant, wash it out, and leave all of the motors in the sun for twenty four hours to dry out before I would test them and decide whether they were usable or needed rewinding. Each piece of equipment was then reassembled, and it was my job to get it working again. We also had to strip and rebuild the main control panels;

the only parts that we had to replace in these, out of the hundreds of contactors and relays, were four timers. We had to replace other parts on some of the machinery. I visited the local electrical wholesaler in Muscat once or twice a week; they had to import some parts from the UK.

The maintenance crew were a mixture of Philippinos and Indians, and they didn't really want us there; they were hoping for new plant, not the old stuff refurbished.

As I explained, my job was to get each piece of plant working, and as I did so I would get it signed off by the insurance assessor and the maintenance manager. On a couple of occasions, I had gotten a piece of machinery working by the end of the day, and the following morning when I came to demonstrate it, it wouldn't work. I learnt from investigation that it had been sabotaged by someone who knew what they were doing. I had my suspicions but bided my time. A few days later I managed to get the most complicated piece of plant working, a pure pack machine. This machine would fold a piece of cardboard into a carton, fill it with milk, and seal it. It combined electrics, air, and Freon gas controls, and I didn't want to have to do it all again. So that afternoon when we left, we parked about a hundred yards up the road and crept back into the dairy, and there was Mohan doing his stuff. Vic had to drag me off him; I think I may have killed him if he hadn't. I only had one more problem with him, and that was on the last day. We had been waiting for some parts from the UK for this last machine, and once finished, I had asked Mohan to set it up to start. It wouldn't start, and I had the insurance assessor and the maintenance manager breathing down my neck, as this was the last thing to be signed off. We also had our flights booked for the following day. I asked Mohan to make sure that he had gotten the settings right, and he swore he had. I pored over the drawings again and identified a relay that was open when it needed to be closed to start the machine. I traced the supply back to one of the gauges that Mohan had set up, and adjusted this. The relay closed and the machine started, and so did I—I once again went for Mohan, who had wasted so much of my time. The insurance assessor calmed me down, as he was already aware of the problems that Mohan had caused previously and had explained this to the manager. I never did find out what happened to him.

Apart from the conditions in which we had to work, I enjoyed the experience and the company of the rest of the team. On one of our days off, three of us drove out to Nizwa, an Oasis, and explored the area. The locals were not very pleased when we wanted to photograph them. The second time, we drove off in the opposite direction; this was during Ramadan. As we wouldn't be able to buy food or drink, we took some with us in a couple of large flasks. We didn't get very far as after a while we ran out of road; it had literally been washed away, and all that was left was desert. The surface was hard, so we drove on and kept seeing bits of road that had been moved, we covered about two miles and came across the road which was intact again, but after a mile or so it had disappeared again, so we turned round and made our way back to the hotel.

On site was also the staff accommodation. We didn't have to do much here apart from the air conditioning units. The one bungalow was still inhabited by the boss and his wife, who were the only Arabs whom we saw on site. We didn't see much of the wife, however, as before we could go into a room in the house, the boss would make sure that his wife was not in there, and would take her to another room if she was. The other man whom we met when he visited was the deputy; he was Tanzanian, and his wife had returned to Zanzibar before the flood. He and his seven-year-old son were sleeping when he got wet and was woken; he had grabbed his son and made his way out onto the road, which was also flooded. Then they had climbed onto the crash barrier and were stranded for many hours until daylight before they were rescued. We were told that many people had died; many were washed away in the flood water, and some bodies were found two kilometres away.

On returning home, I had some jobs waiting for me. One was in Kidderminster at the home of one of the directors of the etching company mentioned earlier. Whilst in the house on my own, there was a knock on the door, which was a guy asking for me. He was from the local garage and had had a phone call asking him to walk the half mile to me and get me to the phone urgently. This was before mobile phones, and there was no phone in the new house. Vic was on the other end; he'd used a lot of detective work to trace me and somehow he'd contacted my wife at her office, who'd contacted Alan, the owner of the house in which I was working. He had then sorted out the phone number of the garage and passed it on to my wife, who relayed it to Vic ,who wanted me to fly to Malta with him the following day for a two-day job.

I did many more jobs for him, including four or five schools in Nottingham, (they were having a spate of arson attacks), a brewery in Leeds, and the Guinness brewery in London. I spent a couple of weeks near Heathrow in a warehouse, sorting out all of the computers that had been manufactured for one of the major supermarkets. They had been stored ready for distribution in a basement, which got flooded.

Shortly afterwards, I was introduced to Kevin, who was MD of a water treatment company. He asked me to design and build some control panels, which were a success, and later he asked to do the same again for some water distillers on skid frames for Iran. I designed and built the panels; the rest of the materials were supplied to me, and I then employed my brother-in-law. Between us, we built three of them and delivered them to Leicester for testing and onward shipment. However, unfortunately the box van that we hired to transport them was not internally high enough to accommodate them, so the top bits had to be stripped off for transporting and rebuilt on delivery.

Oman's Own Dairy

Stand by generator, victim of the flood

Machinery being stripped for cleaning and repair by one of
our team clothed for protection from the searing heat

Hotel Intercontinental, swimming pool

View inland from the hotel

View of Straits of Hormuz and beach with warning sign

HOME AND THE COTTAGES

Where we lived, we had a reasonable-sized garden, and beyond this we had about half an acre of land that belonged to us. This had been left over from when the original owner of the land had sold off all the building plots and had our house built for his daughter, who was my new wife's mother. When I left my first wife, it was not my intention to set up home with Barbara. She had left her parents and was lodging with one of her old tutors, and his wife and wanted a place of her own. Unfortunately, it was the beginning of September, and finding a place to live was almost impossible, as most of the accommodation was already taken by students. A mutual friend told both of us about a vacancy, and we decided to share, so we lived together for eighteen months. Our relationship developed, and when my divorce came through, we decided to marry. Until I was divorced, her parents wanted nothing to do with me, but afterwards we got on really well. It was suggested that we rent this house once we were married, as the present tenants were ready to move on. Meantime, my former wife had remarried, so my previous house was on the market. Once it was sold, we bought this house from Barbara's mother.

We were now regularly visiting the holiday cottage owned by her parents. It was situated outside the village of Aymestrey, Herefordshire in a beautiful part of the country about three-quarter of a mile from the nearest lane, half way up the hill to Croft Ambry, a Roman Hill Fort. I had bought a shotgun, and each morning and evening whilst there I would go out looking for something to shoot, preferably to eat. I had noticed the lack of bird life around, and decided that this was probably due to the number of squirrels with which we were inundated. They would even invade the cottage; we would eliminate them, but next visit they would be in the cottage again, so they became fair game, I personally shot well over a hundred in the first year. My father-in-law and his brother who owned a cottage about half a mile along the track must have shot a similar number, and after a couple of years we noticed that the number of wild birds had increased dramatically. It became a bird watcher's paradise. I also got friendly with the local farmer, Neville, and sorted some electrical problems for him. Then I got more involved in helping on the farm generally, with baling and helping round up the sheep on the hill, amongst other tasks. One day Barbara, her sister Margaret, and I had just arrived in the farmyard with a trailer full of bales, and Nev was talking to another farmer who also happened to be the local squire. The squire was asking him how much he was paying us. Nev said, " I don't pay them; they pay me for the experience." "Tell them they can come and work for me for nothing," the squire said. Nev was joking, but the squire wasn't.

During the dry, hot summer of 1976, the cottage along the track, which had stood there for over four hundred years, suffered from this abnormal heat wave. The external chimney started to part company with the main building, and each week the gap got wider, The owner, John, who was Barbara's uncle, asked me to fix it. I explained that I had no experience in these things and wondered who would be responsible if it collapsed in my attempt to save it. He said that he would not hold me responsible. I did suggest that we use Accros wedged against stakes to support it whilst we dug under the footings a linear foot at a time, as there was no foundations, and then fill it with concrete. He agreed that this seemed the best approach. As it was in the school holidays, I had Margaret, Barbara's sister, staying with us, and also had Malcolm to help. We hired the Accros and a concrete mixer, and Neville loaned us one of his sons to transport the goods to the cottage by tractor, as no other vehicle could have made the journey. We rigged the supports and started to dig; as the first spade full of soil came out, down came the chimney. We were left with a pile of rubble and a hole into the cottage, which I walked through. John had lent me his land rover to gain access across the track, so I used this to go to the farm and phone John to give him the news. All he said was, "You'd better rebuild it then." I explained that I was no builder let alone stoneworker, so we agreed that I should rebuild with blocks and render it. We then hired a small scaffold and bought the blocks, and arranged delivery by way of the tractor again. We cleared away the rubble, dug footings, and started to build a new chimney.

The weather was still scorching. Malcom and I worked in our swimming trunks, and Margaret in her bikini. After a couple of days, Margaret said that she could see someone with binoculars watching her from the wood just below us. I thought she was imagining things until Malcolm saw him. I fetched my shotgun and fired safely into the top of the trees to scare him out, and we saw him run across the open field towards the village, although he was too far away to identify. Barbara wasn't with us during this time, as she had to tend to her own business during the week. The following day was Friday, and she would join us for the weekend. We had arranged to meet her at the local pub and then come back to the cottage for a barbecue. It was dark and we were just settling down to a drink after eating when Margaret said that she could see binoculars in the field below. Out came the gun again, and a shot in the air. The moon was full and we could still see the binoculars reflecting; we made our way closer to discover lots of reflections, a field full of cows' eyes. It took us a while to live that one down. The identity of the original peeping tom was suggested to us, as there had been a previous incident that year with a local lad being the suspect, but no proof.

We managed to complete the job in time for Margaret to go back to school and for me to start another job.

Neville asked me if I could wire one of the barns for lighting on the hill on the opposite side of the road where they did their lambing. Up until now, they had carried out that task by torchlight; there was no mains electricity, but he had bought a generator. I took on the job, and whilst I was up there I noticed a cottage in disrepair with slates missing off the roof. I commented that if something wasn't done about it soon, he would lose it altogether. He said that if I wanted to take on the task of refurbishing it, I could have it as a holiday cottage as long as I paid the rates (council tax).

I thanked him very much, and for the next fourteen years spent every spare weekend there. Considering there was no water, gas, electricity, or sewerage, we made it into a wonderful retreat. And seeing it when it was finished, you would never believe that there were no mains services. We had lighting throughout, full central heating, hot water, a bathroom, complete with shower and bidet, and a full working kitchen. All of this was achieved by doing the following. First we caught the rainwater off the roof and had facilities for storing eight hundred gallons. It was not drinkable, but it fed the hot and cold water system and central heating via a wood burning stove. We were surrounded by a free supply of wood. We had a bank of car batteries that were recharged by a wind generator, which supplied a 12-volt lighting system, and an inverter to convert 12 volts to 230 volts for the heating pump and television. We had a petrol generator for power tools and for pumping the rainwater from the storage barrels to a header tank in the loft. Whenever the generator was run, this was also fed into recharging the batteries. We did have to collect water for drinking and cooking from the farm, but we had two 5-gallon water carriers for this, complete with taps.

We returned from a holiday in St. Lucia in January, and visited the cottage a couple of days later to celebrate one of the local girl's 21st birthday party.

During the evening it started to snow, just the welcome home that one needs after a fortnight of tropical weather. By the time we left the party, there were 3–4 inches of snow, which made our short journey up the track very difficult. By the following morning, the snow was quite deep, leaving us marooned on top of the hill. Fortunately, Nev and his family were also at the party, so they knew that we were in residence and attempted to get to us by tractor. However, they had to return to the farm to fit snow-clearing equipment to clear the track. We eventually managed to negotiate our way down and set off for home.

Whilst working on the cottage roof one day, fixing a cowl to the chimney, I was forced to cling on for dear life as a jet fighter screamed what seemed just above me. I obviously didn't hear it coming, but I felt it overhead. The RAF seemed to use this area a lot due to its sparse population and undulating terrain. I suppose that a cottage on a hill in the middle of nowhere made a good practice target. We often watched them flying in the valley and actually looked down on them.

Later that same day whilst still on the roof, I heard a whoosh as a glider passed just above me and landed in the next field. Shortly afterwards, the pilot came to see me and asked if I owned the field, as apparently he had run out of air and had been forced to land. He had to report this to the landowner and arrange for a tow plane to come and get him up again. I pointed him in the direction of the farm and a while later he returned, explained what the procedure would be, and asked if I would assist. Shortly afterwards, a light plane landed, and they rigged the tow line. My job was to hold the wing of the glider and run with it to make sure that the wing didn't tip and hit the ground. They made a successful take-off, and no doubt made for the local airfield at Shobdon.

During this period, we had cultivated all of the land at the bottom of the garden at home. We grew all of our own vegetables and had taken on a Border Collie pup, "Duke," from the working stock at the farm, along with a pair of geese. Over time we added ducks, chickens, and rabbits. The rabbits were New Zealand Whites, and we bred them commercially. We had five does and one buck; from these, we had around five hundred babies a year. We culled about twenty every fortnight, had regular buyers for them, and ate a lot ourselves. We also bred ducks, chickens, and the geese, which we sold at Christmas. Later, we acquired a bitch, "Sheba," to mate with Duke, and bred from them also. They say that if you don't give a sheepdog a job to do, it will find one. Duke became the sheriff, and took on the job of protecting the birds. When the hens used to squabble or the geese started to throw their weight around, Duke would separate them. The trouble was that he didn't know the difference between fighting and mating, and would even go into the duck pond to stop them from mating. He was a wonderful dog; each evening I only had to say, "Go fetch the geese," and he would round them up and put them in their pen for the night. He did the same with the ducks, but the chicks used to frustrate him as they would fly over him. As dusk came, however, they usually put themselves away.

One day he wouldn't come out of his kennel, which was in the compound; he would growl if we went near. We later discovered that a silky hen was sitting on eggs in there and eventually hatched them. Duke had taken to guarding her. The ducks weren't very good at sitting, so we would put duck eggs under a broody hen. That turned out fine; when they hatched, she would treat them as her own—but got really uptight when they took to the water. Duke would often wander up to the back door of the house, but as soon as a goose or any other bird sounded off, he would go running back to the compound to sort things out. All of the local kids would spend hours watching and sometimes helping with the stock, and they would bring any visitors to see them. On these occasions, Duke would show off by flattening a goose; they were funny to watch, as the geese or the ducks would chase after Duke, being brave until he turned round—and they would then run the opposite way. I've seen him with two or three ducks hanging off his coat, but he never harmed any of them. The only time that I had a problem with him was one Christmas when I had taken a goose into the garage to cull, and it squawked. Duke came running in and had me by the arm; not even I was allowed to harm his birds.

We took the dogs with us on occasions to the cottage, and one time on our return we found that over forty of our birds had been killed by foxes. I tied one of the dead ducklings to a piece of string, then threaded the string over a wild bird feeder in the garden and up through the bedroom window, and tied the other end to the wardrobe door. I put my gun on standby and went to bed; within a few minutes, the wardrobe door flew open. Barbara ran downstairs to turn on the garden lights, and as they came on I could see a fox fighting with the bait on the string. I shot him and put on my dressing gown, went into the garden, and threw the dead fox into the hedge to be sorted in the morning. Then I returned to the bedroom, closed the door, and climbed back into bed. A few minutes later, the door flew open again; this happened four times in the first hour, and I had killed four foxes—but I had to be on the six o'clock train to London the following morning, so decided to call it a day, or night. Over ten days, I killed fourteen foxes. I started burying them, but found that the foxes were digging them up again, so I started putting each of them into a large empty feed bag to take to the local tip. I had ten of them in the back of the car as well as a young neighbour, Stephen, who had become a regular helper. As we were unloading them, I noticed that there was a man looking through the rubbish for anything worth having. He had spotted us throwing these bags in and headed our way. I called to Steve to get in the car so that we could get out of there before he opened those bags. I wish now that I'd waited to see the look on his face when he discovered his find.

Shortly afterwards, I was listening to the radio whilst driving to a job, and the presenter was saying something about urban foxes. He wanted people to ring in regarding a fox watch, and gave a telephone number. I got my passenger to write down the number, and later I rang in. I explained to the guy on the other end that I lived on the outskirts of the city and had seen fourteen foxes in my garden in ten days. "Really?" he said sarcastically, "and how do you know that they were fourteen different foxes?" "Because I shot them dead," I replied. He put the phone down on me.

Tractors to the rescue

Making our way back to civilization

The glider that landed in the next field

The cottage with temporary roof repairs

The sitting room of the cottage when we took it over

The same sitting room after refurbishment

Sheba and Duke

A NEW OPENING

Barbara and I returned from one of our holidays in Tenerife and found a message waiting for me to ring Paul Taylor, who I had known through one of the wholesalers with whom I had dealt. He had now moved to a company named Switchplan, newly formed from the remnants of the control panel manufacturers Floorplan, which I had previously sub contracted to. Now they were into automated lighting controls. He asked me to meet him at their offices to see what they were doing, with a view to doing some work for them. After showing me the lighting panels and giving me a demonstration, he asked me to do a day's work in London for them. I agreed, and that day's work lasted over ten years. At the time, they had two projects, both in London, and I was asked to complete the installations and commission them. By the time that I had completed them, they had a dozen more, including one in Glasgow. I travelled to London on the 6.05 a.m. train each morning and arrived home at about 9.30 p.m. One day I left home at 4 a.m. to pick up Paul and the same MD Dave as before, and drove to Glasgow to complete the job on time. We left for home at 11.30 p.m., dropping off Paul and Dave the MD, and arranged to meet the following evening at one of the projects in London that was running late, to work through the night. I arrived home from Glasgow at about 5 a.m., then caught the 7.05 a.m. train to London, as I had another project running late. I worked all day on this project and set off to meet the others at 7 p.m., to learn that they had had the day off. This tight schedule didn't improve over the next two years. I was being run ragged, but the financial rewards were okay, so I stuck at it until I got to the point of an increase of work with which I couldn't cope on my own, and asked if they would pay for me to take on more labour. At first they employed someone to work with me. However, it didn't work out, as he was expecting to work normal hours, not the 14–15 hours a day including travelling, so they left me to run the site department and invoice them accordingly.

Whilst working on one of the building sites opposite the Old Bailey, I was travelling in the lift on my own when it stopped between floors due to a power failure to the building. There should have been an emergency light in the lift, but someone obviously hadn't carried out their maintenance, so all I could do was wait and hope in the pitch dark. After about five minutes, I heard someone above shouting, "Is there anyone in the lift?" I let them know that there was only me. "What floor are you stuck at?" "Somewhere between ground and twelve, I haven't really got a clue." They eventually found me and opened the outer, then inner doors. There was about an 18-inch gap between the floor level and the top of the lift. They relieved me of my tools, and two of them lay on the floor and leant in to grab my arms to pull me out.

Not a pleasant experience, good job I didn't suffer from claustrophobia.

One morning, Barbara was about to drive me to the station when I noticed that Duke wasn't in the compound but rather was lying by the garage door. As we were running late, we left him there for Barbara to sort out after she had dropped me off. When she got back, she realized that he wasn't very well and, on investigation, noticed blood on his chest, so she took him to the vets. It seems that he had been stabbed, and we learned later that day that two houses had been burgled. We can only assume that he disturbed the burglar, as he rarely barked but would go to investigate anything strange. He did make a good recovery but was never quite so agile again.

CONFRONTATIONS

Working on site most of the time was, to say the least, 'challenging.'

Apart from the confrontations mentioned separately, there were many more on sites with Project managers, consultants, and even Switchplan management.

We spent about three years involved with the Shell building whilst it was being refurbished, and with many more on completion of that, having won the maintenance contract for the lighting control system.

When a water main burst on the top floor and flooded one electrical riser, writing off two of the eight lighting control panels on each of the eight floors, we won the contract to replace them, much to the annoyance of the Switchplan management, who reluctantly agreed to supply us with replacements. I suppose contractually they had no choice.

The system was controlled by a central computer, which designated which lights would switch on and off and at what time. Most of the lighting also had local switch control but would still be switched off in phases by the computer. However, the corridor lighting had no local control and was switched on and off at specific times. Saturday and Sunday the corridor lights were not timed to switch on, leaving just the few 24-hour lights for safety.

One of my rare free Saturdays, I had a phone call from the project manager, a Mr. Peacock of Matthew Hall, who were the main contractors for the Shell refurbishment.

"We have a problem with your lighting controls."

"What is the problem?"

"We can't get the corridor lights off on the sixth floor, and we can't get a lot of the office lighting on."

"Have you checked the circuit breakers for the office lighting, and have you checked that no one has linked out the terminals on the corridor lights in the lighting control panel?" (This is a practice by maintenance staff, to get lighting on when working out of hours.)

"Do you think I'm stupid or something? I am an electrical engineer; just get down here and sort it out."

A few hours later, having taken the train from Birmingham to London, I arrived on site to find that Mr. Peacock was unavailable, so I went in search of Chagger, his Indian understudy. Once I found him, I asked him to accompany me to the problem area. I then asked him to open the riser and witness that I touched nothing, but had carried out a visual check. I then asked him to fetch Mr. Peacock. Chagger also told me that Peacock was unavailable. I then got very annoyed and demanded that he get him and let him know that a very irate Rick Harris wanted urgently to see him. He eventually arrived and asked who I thought I was, demanding to see him. I answered, "You demanded that I get down here and sort out my non existent problems, take a look for yourself. 'Circuit breakers, off.' "I think you will find that if you switch them on, your lights will work. Links in the terminals holding corridor lights on—I didn't put those links in so not my problem. The situation is exactly as I suggested on the phone. I now want an order to cover me for a day's work and my travel expenses. Next time don't be so pig-headed, listen, and save your company some money." By this time we had an audience, and he was fuming but speechless.

All of this had been to get his revenge from two previous encounters. Once was when there had been a problem in the chairman's office. He said I couldn't go in whilst the chairman was in there, but I had just pushed past and asked the chairman's secretary for permission to enter, just as the chairman came to speak to his secretary. "Ah, just the man, come in," he said. That hadn't gone down too well. On another occasion, he was trying to put me down in the company of one of the consultants who was asking me how the job was going. "This is Rick Harris, the commissioning engineer for the Switchplan lighting control system," Said Peacock, "Don't worry I'll keep an eye on things; when Matthew Hall says jump, Switchplan will jump." I replied, lying, "The only reason that I'm here is not to make a living, but to keep out of my wife's way while she earns more than enough for both of us. The only jumping I will be doing is on the train home, so if you want the job completed, I'd zip it." The consultant's comment when I saw him later was, "He doesn't like you very much does he? I think he's a little pissed with power."

We had completed the commissioning at Confederation Life in Stevenage, and the client asked for some modifications to be carried out to a number of the individual offices before the staff moved in. The MD of Switchplan, because of the urgency, instructed me to take two of my men and stay on site until the work was completed. Half way through the job, I was called to the site office to take a call from Paul, the MD's understudy. He gave instructions that one of us had to leave site, travel to London, and meet the two design engineers from Switchplan at Euston station when they arrived. We were to show them the way to Merryl Lynch, a project that we had completed but had a design fault on the computer that needed their expertise. "No one ever showed me the way to any of the sites that I had been asked to visit. Many of them offered very little information—so why did they need an escort?" I asked.

I offered to give directions and explained that we were under a great deal of pressure, working all hours to complete the job here, and that time was running out. "So you're refusing to go then," Paul suggested. I wasn't, but now that it had been suggested, I said, "Yes." He then hung up. We completed the work on the Sunday night before the staff moved in on Monday.

On that Monday, we went to our designated jobs, and I rang the office to inform them that we had completed the modifications at Confederation Life and to update them on the other projects that we were working on. Paul came on the line. "Dave (The MD) wants a word with you." I decided to get in first. I put the same argument to Dave, and reminded him that his instructions had been to stay on site until the mods were completed. "What am I supposed to do when I get different instructions from different people? Not only that, but running from one job to another and back again is grossly inefficient and costly; you have asked me to try to keep the costs down. I'm trying, but I also need your support." He wasn't happy, but didn't have much of an argument. He didn't apologise, but did thank me for completing on time.

A passive infra red system of controlling the lighting was installed at Glaxo.

Each bank of lights would be controlled by one or two sensors. As personnel moved into the area, lights would automatically switch on, and when the area was vacated, the lights would switch off shortly afterwards.

Combined with this was the corridor lighting. When the first sensor was activated in a given zone, in addition to switching on its individual area, it would also switch on the corridor lighting. When the last of the area lighting switched off, the corridor lighting was designed to switch off soon afterwards. Part of the commissioning procedure was to ensure that this did happen. I noted that when all of the zone lighting had switched off, the corridor lighting also switched off as it should, but it triggered a lot of the sensors, bringing the lights back on again. I suspected that the electrical noise created by all of the corridor lights switching off together was causing this problem and decided that the sensors needed screening. To prove the point, I sent one of the lads out to purchase a roll of kitchen foil, which we wrapped around some of the sensors being triggered and connected the foil screen to earth. On the next test, the only sensors to trigger were the ones not screened. We carried out the same test a number of times and verified that this was the problem and the solution. As it was not ethical or professional to screen in this way, I decided to ask the MD to visit the site as a matter of urgency to witness the problem for himself. I preferred to do this before suggesting that all of the sensors be returned to the factory, and the housings be sent for chrome plating, and an earth connection be fitted. Once again, he was not a happy man, but he at least appreciated that I had found the solution as well as the problem. The production manager was not so appreciative. He rang me and gave me an earful, as he was having trouble meeting his output target as it was. Now I was having him send 50 percent of his output back for refurbishment, plus what was at the works ready for despatch. You would think that I had created the fault. I was only doing what I was paid to do.

The production manager, Ken, was also the design engineer. Whilst working at Standard Chartered Bank, I installed an active infra red call system in each of the senior directors' offices, Ken had designed these, but I couldn't get them to work and called him to site to rectify the fault. Ken didn't like being wrong and certainly would never admit it. I took him to one of the faulty receivers mounted on the wall, which needed steps to reach. He stood on the steps and spent some time working on it. I couldn't see what he was doing, but he did do some soldering. Once it was working, he said, "No problem; you had made a simple wiring mistake, which I have corrected." "That's OKAY," I said, "I'll check what wiring correction you have made and correct the other five that don't work." "Ah, um, no I'll do it now that I'm here," he said. "You mean you'll fit the extra component that's missing?" I taunted. "Ah! You noticed."

This wasn't the first time that this kind of thing had happened—why do people like that keep digging holes for themselves?

On the subject of Standard Charter, the site PM (project manager), Mr Armiger, another Matthew Hall man, was an impossible man to get on with. During construction of the building, his office was in the basement three floors below ground, and there were eight floors above ground. I had a riser to work in on each of the floors, and a lot of the work was wiring between risers. There were no lifts, and he would only allow me a key to one riser at a time. This meant that I spent most of my day walking up and down flights of stairs. Each time I returned a key, I would try to explain how futile this situation was. The following day, I decided I would sort it. I walked into his office and demanded keys for floors eight, seven, six, and five. He gave me one for floor eight. I once again pointed out to him that not only was this performance tiring, it was also time consuming. As the company for which I was working was on a fixed price for the contract, I was sure that no financial consideration for all of this time wasting had been made—so could we negotiate it now? He thumped his desk and told me to get out of his office. I thumped his desk in return and said, "Not until we have agreed on a price for this time wasting, or you give me at least four keys at a time so that I can work efficiently, or I could leave site." "I think you'd better leave site," He said.

"I'll write to Switchplan and to your head office to explain my reasons for leaving," I said.

When I got to Euston Station, I rang the MD to let him know what had happened, but he already knew and wasn't happy with me, as Matthew Hall was his biggest client. I did tell him my side of the story and impressed upon him the cost implications etc., and suggested that he take it up with someone in the contract's department at MH head office. After all, I was only acting in his financial interests and in the interest of getting the job done.

He suggested that I ring him again when I got home.

I don't know what was said in the meantime, but when I rang him late that afternoon, I was told that I would be given a complete set of keys the following day, as long as I signed for and returned them at the end of each day, which was the general rule anyway. When I arrived on site the following day, I didn't have to face the PM, as the keys were now kept in a different office under the supervision of one of his staff. I didn't see him again for a while, and I must admit that I didn't go looking for him. The story had obviously gotten around, as we hadn't been alone in his office. One of his staff whom I knew from a previous project asked if it was true that I had been in the navy. I told him that it was true."Weren't you also a *Ganges* boy?" he asked. I confirmed that I was."Well if you've experienced that, then why are you avoiding Armiger? He was only a batman in the army—are you frightened of him?" "No," I said, "I'm frightened of what I might do to him," I joked. "Ah, now I understand," he said.

Whilst commissioning at The Daily Express building, I attended a meeting with the client, consultant, and contractors over a dispute on how the lighting system had been configured. The problem was mainly with the consultant, who didn't seem to completely understand what the client wanted or what he had specified. In conversation with him afterwards, when he was trying to offload the blame, I suggested that he, being a consultant, should learn to do just that, 'consult,' preferably with someone who understood how the system should work.

Shortly after my son started working for me, I took him to Lloyds Bank, Hays Galleria. The installation had been completed by contractors, who were now in a hurry to get the job handed over. On switching on the power, 90 percent of the system showed no life. After carrying out a few tests, I discovered that we had no '0 volt' at the receivers. Since it was a 12 volt system, we relied on the earth for the '0 volt'. We traced one of the faults to an earth cable lying in the cable trunking, where the installers seemed to have run out of cable and had not connected it to the next run of cable. I then decided that, as we had other projects demanding our attention, we were not going to spend our time tracing faults created by others and reported the problem to the PM. He told me that it was my job to commission, and that included finding and rectifying faults. "Yes," I said. "Rectifying faults to our equipment, not to the installation; that surely is your problem. I've told you what the faults are, and I'll even show you the one we have traced and rectified, but we're now leaving site. Ring the office when you have rectified the rest of them." During the ensuing argument, my son joined in. I told him to "Shut up and wait outside." I then asked the PM if I could use his phone to speak to my MD to get a decision. The MD at first said that we should stay, until I told him that it could take days to trace all of the faults. He then agreed with me, before speaking to the PM, and we left site.

There were many occasions like the above, but to finish on a lighter note: The refurbishment of the Canadian High Commission had been carried out on a floor-by-floor basis, but the commissioning was carried out when the staff was in residence. Part of the commissioning procedure on this occasion was to visit every office, remove part of each light fitting to access the receiver, and code it. I was working in a senior army officer's office and being questioned by him, when he opened the adjoining door to the office belonging to an Admiral, that I had previously visited, when I heard him say. "Hey Admiral, have you met this guy fixing these lights, has he been vetted, he could be planting bugs in our offices for all we know." "I think, General, that the procedure is that everyone is screened before being allowed to work here ."

These were but a few of the confrontations, and I could have done without them, but on reflection I suppose that they did provide a little entertainment.

HOLIDAYS

Most years we had two foreign holidays, one of which was usually Teneriffe. One holiday in St. Lucia at a Cunard Hotel, we were invited aboard one of the cruise liners for the day whilst she was in Castries harbour. We were enjoying ourselves so much that we lost track of time and didn't realize that the rest of the party had left the ship. Then I noticed that the ship was getting ready to sail, and we had to quickly change from swimming gear, rush to find the rest of our belongings, and get off the ship. It was almost like my experience on the submarine Token again. Me going one way and the Captain the other.

The following year, we visited Mauritious. On arrival, we discovered that one of our cases had gone missing. The hotel rules at the time were that ties must be worn at dinner. The missing case contained all of our evening clothes, so neither of us had anything to wear for dinner. We approached the hotel management who already knew of the missing case. They made an exception in our case, but suggested that we purchase something from the beach market traders. The only shirts that I could find were holiday shirts—no ties or trousers. Barbara bought a one-piece dress, which was more of a strange-shaped piece of material that could be worn in different ways. We stuck out like sore thumbs on the first night, with me in shorts and a shirt with a slogan on the back, and Barbara with a dress pinned together. We made a visit to the capital, St. Louis, the following day when our case still hadn't turned up. Barbara managed to find a couple of respectable dresses that needed alterations, and I found a pair of trousers that also had to be altered. All would be ready in a couple of days, but anything other than holiday shirts had to be made to measure and would take a week. As we had been assured that our case would turn up within the next few days, I didn't bother with a shirt. We eventually had our case delivered to our home, a month after we returned from our holiday. Meanwhile we dressed the best that we could. Apart from that, we had a wonderful holiday, spending a lot of time sailing and water skiing. We were considering returning the following year or visiting the Maldives but it wasn't to be.

A few years previously, Barbara had, with my help, set up her own accounting and bookkeeping business, first working from home. As the business developed, however, we bought office premises and did very well; she employed five staff, and all seemed to be fine until one day I saw her being driven past me in her car. When I confronted her, she said that one of her clients had ran out of petrol and that she had gone to his aid. Really? Why was he driving her car? I also learned he wasn't the first, so we split up and she left home. She did ask if we could try again, but I would never have been able to trust her.

Once again, I felt like I was starting again from scratch. I couldn't cope with all of the animals on my own, with the amount of travelling that I was doing, so I had to get rid of all of them except for Duke.

I lived on my own for the next twelve months and, like any other single feller, I made the most of it. I eventually met a lady by the name of Tina, a vegetarian who hardly ate anything but was as strong as an ox. She was a sales rep and her parents were farmers, so I'd spend my weekends working on the farm with her. We went to Gran Canaria for a holiday, but as she didn't eat much, she had to put up with sitting and watching me eat out every night. All she wanted was a bit of cheese and lettuce; trying to find somewhere for her to eat was a nightmare.

One day, we had arranged to go on a jeep safari. I asked if we would be driving ourselves, and was told that the terrain that we would be driving over would take the expertise of their drivers and that I would not be experienced enough. We stopped for breakfast on the way, and the place where we stopped didn't cater for vegetarians. All Tina had was a cup of tea; the rest of us had a full English.

Later, while driving over some rough terrain in the mountains, we dipped into a valley and, as it had been raining recently, here we ended up in what seemed like a very muddy field. There were five jeeps with six passengers in each driving in line abreast. It wasn't long before we were all stuck, and our driver was trying forward and reverse to no avail. I suggested that he engage 4-wheel drive, but he said that he knew what he was doing and was already in 4-wheel drive. "Well, why is only one wheel out of four spinning?" I asked. Then I realised that the vehicles had free-wheeling hubs. I asked him to wait, and asked one of the other passengers to hold my legs as I lay on the bonnet and leant over and locked the hubs on both front wheels, "Try now," I suggested, and we moved out. The driver shouted something in Spanish to the other drivers, and they eventually followed. So much for not being experienced enough, and so much for their expertise. The holiday itself with Tina made me realise that we had no future, and we parted ways.

ANOTHER SPLIT

I eventually had about ten men working for me, including my son. We were having a problem on one particular project, mainly because of a lack of equipment; we were under pressure to complete, as the job was due for handover to the client. I asked for a meeting with the MD to see what could be done about it. Because of my split with Barbara, my brain wasn't functioning as it should, so I asked my son to attend the meeting with me and gave him a few prompts to give me should I get lost. As it happened, I didn't need them, as once I got started there was no stopping me. The MD couldn't make the meeting, so his deputy, Paul, stood in. I asked the production manager how long this particular project had been on the books.

"Over twelve months," he said. I already knew this, as we had started on site nine months previously. "When was the material that we are short of due in?" "End of next week." "When was it ordered?" He looked through his papers, "Two weeks ago." "Why not sooner?" "Not being a production manager, you wouldn't understand." "Ken, do you know what my last job was before I went self employed?" "No, Rick, I don't." "Production Manager." He stood up and said, "I don't have to put up with this from a sub contractor," and stormed out, got in his car, and went home. The MD was called in and told of the situation. I wasn't very popular but I did say that being at the sharp end on site, I got this treatment every day and I hadn't stormed off. The MD had to drive to Ken's home to talk him into returning to work.

I was asked by many of the clients to arrange maintenance contracts for the systems that we had commissioned. I passed this information to the MD, but nothing was ever done and it became embarrassing to meet the clients again and have them complain of the inefficiency of the company. So I decided to take on the maintenance contracts myself. This became quite lucrative, the only drawback being that the work had to be carried out over the weekends. However, with the extra labour that I now employed, it wasn't too much of a strain. Certain jobs only I could do, as they were the earlier systems and no one else understood them. I made my son a partner in the business and gave him a 40 percent share. The MD came to realise that he had missed out on this lucrative business, and at one of our meetings he dictated that all maintenance contracts would be carried out through his office. I told him that he had no right to the contracts, and that if he wanted them, he would have to tender for them—and who would he get to do them anyway? Shortly afterwards, he employed someone in house from another lighting control company to run the commissioning, taking the responsibility from me. This was his first step in his bid to get rid of me. This new man made the mistake of giving my employees their instructions on where and when they were to work without consulting me; he also tried to poach them from me, and things became rather tense, and another argument between myself and the MD took place. During this time, I had approached him with what I considered to be a much simpler control system, which I suggested that he should develop. He didn't agree, so with this in mind, I quit. So did my son, and we decided to go it alone; with all of the maintenance contracts that we had, we would have time and money to develop our own system. I contacted a guy that I knew of and asked if he could help with the design; we produced an intelligent, passive, infra red sensor to control office lighting. It was very successful, and I estimated that we had about two years before someone else would copy it or come up with something similar. As it turned out, we had less time than that before fate dealt another blow …

MEANWHILE

Shortly after parting from Tina, I was introduced to Carol, and soon after that to her nine-year-old daughter, Julie. After about three years of living together, we got married. I didn't realise at the time that I was getting a whole package—wife, daughter, another dog Sally the Springer, hamster, budgie, and eventually mother- and father-in-law plus another budgie.

Carol and Julie say that they bought me at a car boot sale.

After Carol and Julie had moved in with me, I was refurbishing a bedroom for Julie and had to collect some materials that I had ordered from a place in Sparkbrook. When I arrived at the place, I parked in one of the side streets. I got out of the car and heard a voice through a loud hailer shout, "This is the police; get back in your car, lock the doors, and stay there." The voice came from a helicopter hovering just above me. I cracked open the window so that I could hear what was going on and waited. An eternity later, I heard a gunshot, then shortly afterwards I heard, "You may now leave your vehicles." Apparently, there had been an armed bank robbery a few minutes before I arrived, a few yards from where I had parked. One of the armed robbers was on the loose and was finally shot.

*****

Whilst we were organising the manufacture of the sensors and the ancillary equipment, we decided to do what I had wanted to do for many years, and that was to move to Herefordshire. We were staying at our holiday cottage during the school half term; my son was also with us with his partner Christine and his daughter Sandra. We'd gone into Leominster and had had lunch in one of the many hostelries, and as we were walking back to the car it started to pour with rain. We stepped into an estate agents to keep dry, and whilst browsing, we spotted the house that would suit all of our needs and arranged a viewing.

With a few modifications, we would be able to accommodate Carol's elderly parents, Tom and Maud, without them imposing on our privacy. They would have their own space: bedroom, living room, kitchen, and bathroom. I built ramps and fitted other disabled facilities for Tom, who was wheelchair-bound.

We also had plenty of space for an office as well as for a workshop for the business. The property stood in two-thirds of an acre of beautiful, parkland-type garden. It took twelve months to move in, as the sale of our house fell through twice.

DUKE AND BLUE

We moved in May, and of course Duke, now fourteen, moved in with us. I spent a month carrying out the modifications to Carol's parents' new accommodation, and they moved in during June. Duke had a further happy twelve months before he started to show his age, then over the next year he became dependant on tablets to keep him alive. As we lived upstairs, this also meant me carrying him up and down regularly, and he was rather a large dog. He would let me pick him up and carry him up or down, but each time I put him down again, he would growl, as if to say, "I can manage, thank you." Still proud. Some of the memories we have of him are the way that he tried to talk. With a little help holding his mouth, we could have a short conversation with him.

Me: "Who loves you duke?"

Duke: "Mommy."

Me: "Whose Mommy?"

Duke: "My Mommy."

Another memory was the way that he would play ball. I would throw a large ball to him, and he would use his nose to bounce it back to me; I would tire first.

Clearing the drive of snow, he would catch every shovel full.

If there was a football match going on, or any game, he had to join in.

Shortly before he had a stroke, he was in the garden when a flock of sheep ventured in. He stood there mesmerised; I think he thought he had died and gone to heaven.

We were all so upset when he died a month short of his sixteenth birthday that I said I wouldn't have another, but shortly afterwards, Julie decided that she wanted a puppy—and who was I to refuse her? She would look after it and walk it etc. etc. If she didn't, mother would. Who ended up doing most of it? Me.

We eventually settled on a blue roan Sprocker (a cross between a Springer and a Cocker spaniel). His mother had been a liver and white Springer, and his father a blue roan Cocker from working stock. We'd decided on this breed, thinking it would turn out quite small and that when the time came for me to carry it up and down stairs in my advancing years, he wouldn't be too difficult to handle. We had the choice out of a litter of six; he chose us. I think he could read "sucker" written on our foreheads. He came trotting towards us and demanded to come with us; how could we refuse? Within a few minutes, Julie said, "Can we name him Blue?" It was an ideal name, as he was at that time very blue. He eventually grew to the size of a large Springer.

After Duke, who had been a well-behaved, real gentleman, I don't know how Blue survived the first six months. His ambition seemed to be to play havoc with everything and everybody. When Maud would be using the mop or broom, we'd hear the cry for help. "Rick, Carol, get this dog off my broom. Now he's pinched my dusters." From Tom it would be, "Blue has pinched my glasses," or his slippers off his feet. Blue would always want to go out at about ten to nine each morning and would disappear until one of the local children would bring him back. It was a while before we realised that he had loads of friends at the village school and would go to meet them each morning, and they would take it in turns bringing him back. Most of the kids didn't know us at first, but they all knew Blue. When he was eighteen months old, I took him beating for the first time, and he took to it like a duck to water. I just had to teach him a little control, and he soon became top dog. If for some reason I couldn't make it, the keeper would ask, "Can you still send your dog?" His only problem was that he was too enthusiastic; most dogs would take it easy between drives, but he would never stop; he just kept hunting. He loved all aspects of working, whether it was beating, picking up for me if I was shooting, or searching for shot birds that had gotten lost in the wood. He was also good at fetching ducks that had been shot and landed in the water; he would even go into the water to try to put them up, but most times the ducks could swim faster than he.

One day between drives we were walking alongside a wood towards our transport to the next drive, and he must have spotted a pheasant in the wood. He jumped over the fence but didn't quite make it, and he got hooked up on the barbed wire. As I ran towards him, I could see his stomach being ripped open, and even then he wanted to carry on hunting with his insides hanging out.

After he had been stitched up by the vet, he was quite poorly for a few days, but as soon as he started to feel better, he made my life very difficult. He didn't understand that it would be about six weeks before he would be able to work again, and whenever I was in the house, his eyes would never leave me in case I should show signs of preparing to go out. We hatched elaborate plans for me to continue beating or shooting. On one occasion, I had to walk down the stairs backwards with my gun wrapped up in a coat in front of me and go into my office at the far end of the house and sit at my desk. Once convinced, he would wander back to other company. Just to reassure him, I would go back upstairs, have a chat to Carol, and then return to the office, Blue watching every move. I would then leave through the patio door. I would walk to my car, which Carol had earlier parked at the bottom of the drive, and go off for the day. If he suspected that I had gone shooting without him, he would howl until I returned.

Once a week, an ambulance-type vehicle would arrive to take Tom to the village hall to Age Concern. Cliff, the driver, would lower the chair lift at the back to load Tom. Blue would be in there greeting the other passengers and looking for something to take that Cliff would spend the next ten minutes trying to retrieve, usually his gloves.

He knew his routines, and one was that if he had been walking and got wet, he would go into the workshop, jump on the bench, and wait to be towelled dry. One day one of the child neighbours had taken him on a walk whilst we were out, and on his return, Blue pestered Tom, who was in his wheelchair, until he followed him into the workshop. Blue pointed out the towel with his nose before jumping onto the bench. Tom's comment when we got back was, "I wouldn't mind, but he wasn't even wet."

He would always accompany us on our walks with the village walking group, and I believe he was liked by all. One day whilst walking with the group, he turned up with a pheasant and, as normal, he presented it to me. I felt a little embarrassed until on inspection I realised that although it was still alive, it had been previously shot and couldn't fly anyway. Soon afterwards, the group split up; some would take the shortcut back to the vehicles whilst others would walk the longer way. Greta, one of the ladies taking the shortcut, offered to carry the now dead bird back for me.

Whenever I was walking with him, I rarely had to use the lead. He became very obedient and always responded to my whistle and other instructions, except at home in the company of visitors. For example, when we ran the Bed and Breakfast, he wasn't allowed in the guests' accommodation. Yet they would often invite him in, as most of them fell in love with him, and he would sit on their feet and look at me as if to say, "Now tell me to leave." One of the comments left in the guest book was, "Lovely house, nice people, **great dog**."

Our postman, when delivering our post, would walk in, make a fuss of Blue, who would be lying on the landing waiting for him, then leave the post and take any outgoing mail that we had left on the landing. We also had a lady working for us, and any mail that she had to post she would bring to leave with ours, Blue would sort hers out and remove it. When we moved into the new house, the same postman trained Blue to take the post from him and would send him to me with it.

Sadly, like the rest of us, he aged. He was still a pup at the age of twelve and still looked a pup, but he started to have health problems and then a stroke. From then on, although still seemingly happy, he had difficulty walking without falling over. Months previously, we had booked to have a month's holiday in January and, having consulted with our wonderful vet, we left him with my sister and her husband, who did an excellent job of looking after him and reported to us by text regularly. He had settled in with them and when we returned, he seemed quite relaxed, although excited when he spotted us. It seemed as though he had been waiting for us to come home, as within a few days he deteriorated. The Monday after we returned from our holiday, he couldn't stand at all. We called in the vet, who informed us that he had done all that he could do. We arranged for him to be cremated so that we could scatter his ashes over Hergest, his favourite playground. All dogs are special to their owners, but once in a while an extra-special one comes along. Blue was one of those "one in a million."

Julie aged twelve with Duke

Blue

Blue doing what he loved doing most

Another of his favourites, playing with the hamster in his ball

Blue, or is it Oliver? "Please can I have some more?"

It's Christmas day, present opening time

A NEW VENTURE

When we first went into the production of our new lighting control system, we were inundated with contracts, some new, and some to replace older Switchplan systems that I had previously installed or commissioned. We would have a meeting with the client, take all of their relevant details such as office working hours, number of light fittings and wattages, etc., and work out a payback period for the installation of our lighting controls. Payback was usually an average of eighteen months. Our first major order was for eight floors of the Sedgwick Centre next to Aldgate East tube station, worth a quarter-million pounds. This had also been my first major commissioning contract for Switchplan. We learnt later that our system was saving the client six hundred pounds per floor per week, giving a payback period of twelve months for materials and the installation cost of fifteen thousand pounds another three weeks. The client was obviously over the moon. We also won the contract to supply and install for Bankers Trust, in the Broadgate centre sited around Liverpool Street Station. We supplied the materials and subcontracted the installation. We did the same for a the DTI building in Buckingham Palace road. We did have to fight for an order from Lehman Brothers. I had been involved with this building since it had been built as one of the first in the Broadgate Centre. We had been told verbally that we had gotten the contract to refurbish two floors, and then we were called to a meeting with the client and one of their employed architects, who was also their nominated project manager, to sort out the final details. The architect put up all sorts of obstacles for us, one being the colour of our sensor, which didn't quite match the colour of their ceiling tiles. I agreed that we could arrange to do this, and he then tried another tack and I got suspicious. It was obvious that he didn't want us to have the order, so I asked who we were in competition with. He wouldn't say, but the client did; it was Switchplan. The client also asked about if Switchplan got the job—would they also be asked to change the colour of their sensor? He said that he had always had problems with Switchplan management, and that it was always my company that had come to the rescue, and he demanded that we be given the order. The architect had obviously been gotten at by Switchplan's MD, and he was fighting his corner, or for his backhander. We had maintained this building for about ten years and continued to do so for many years afterwards.

As I said, it wasn't initially someone copying the idea that slowed the sales; it was after about six months that the electricity generating companies were privatised, and high users of energy could then haggle for cheaper electricity. When we started, the price was between five and six pence per KW hour, allowing us to give a payback period of one to two years. On privatisation, the price for these high users dropped to two pence, pushing the payback period to four or five years, and customers were not so keen to invest their funds for so long a payback. Work still came in, but clients were now not so enthusiastic and the projects not so large.

We were still kept busy, and still had many maintenance contracts. The following are a few of the memorable experiences. We had worked all night at Glaxo near Heathrow, and just got into bed in the hotel when the phone rang. It was a guy from Britoil in Glasgow asking for urgent attention, as the whole building had gone into disco effect, lights flashing on and off every second, and the staff had to be evacuated. This was a Switchplan system that we still maintained. I caught a flight to Glasgow and asked a few questions of the maintenance staff to see if any work had been carried out that may help pinpoint the whereabouts of the fault. Not much help, so I decided to check the connections at all of the twenty or so control stations and, luckily, found the problem at the first one I looked at. Someone had been a little heavy handed whilst working in the riser and put some weight on the incoming data cable, pulling one of the five cores out of its connector and shorting to another.

The only flight back was at five o'clock, so I had a long wait. On arriving back at Heathrow it was back to Glaxo for a site meeting before working through the night again.

It was here at Glaxo that I made the only nearly catastrophic mistake of my career. I'd gotten three or four lads working with me fitting our sensors; some would be removing the large ceiling tiles to be drilled with a 57 mm hole saw, others fitting and testing the sensors and replacing the tiles. I was drilling the holes in the tiles, we had dust sheets in the immediate area of work, and I had a trestle to lay each tile on to be drilled. To make the cutting easier and to prolong the life of the cutter, I used metal cutting paste, which was in a large tin alongside the trestle. Whilst cutting, I would lift the driller holding the cutter, and would dunk it in the paste; however, one time the cutter was still spinning quite fast when it caught the side of the tin and threw it in the air, and the sticky paste went everywhere—on the ceiling, carpet, walls, and desks. We spent the next couple of hours cleaning up; fortunately, a friendly security guard knew where the spare carpet tiles were stored and let me change the badly soiled ones. We must have done a good job, as we never had any complaints.

*****

We'd gone to London, as we did on most Saturday mornings, and arranged to meet a couple of other guys who were working for us. We'd delivered a load of equipment to Lehman Brothers via their underground car park loading bay, left the van there, then went to Liverpool Street railway station cafeteria to meet the others. As they arrived, we were cleared out because of a bomb threat. We ran back to our van to get it out before we were barred from there as well, then met up again with the other lads to hand over their instructions and materials for a job just round the corner in Copthall Avenue. We ourselves had a few maintenance jobs to carry out over the weekend. Our first call was to be Zurich in Fenchurch Street, which meant driving the few yards to Moorgate, turning left onto London Wall, going down past the Baltic Exchange and into Fenchurch Street. We had just turned into Moorgate and passed Moorgate tube station and were sitting in stationary traffic outside the Zagreb Bank when there was a terrific bang. My first thought was that we had been hit by another vehicle, as the van was picked up and turned facing the bank. Then we were hit by the falling shattered windows and other debris, and I realised that it was a bomb. I suggested to David that he use any means possible to get away from there in case there was another one; meanwhile I dialled 999 on my then rather large mobile. I hung on for ages with no answer, and by this time we were crossing London Wall as we were stopped by the police from turning left into it. I then decided that with the amount of police presence, my call wouldn't tell them much so I hung up. Soon afterwards, the phone rang and I got a rollicking for hanging up on the emergency services. When asked, I told of our recent experience and said it was the bank that had been bombed, which at the time was what I thought. Later, of course, we learnt that it was the Baltic Exchange, the first of the IRA's big bombs, although on the news it did say that there was a second bomb at the Zagreb Bank. However, that turned out to not be true; I think it was my report that that had gotten into the media. The damage around the area was horrific. We had been two hundred yards away, and that was terrifying. Even sheltered by many other buildings, our ears were ringing for the next few days.

As we could not now go to Zurich or any of the two other jobs in the area, we decided to cross the river and head for the two jobs that we had lined up for the Sunday. With the chaos around and some of the bridges closed, it took us a while to reach the Canadian Imperial Bank. When we arrived, we were surprised to learn that the blast was felt even across the water, enough to pop some of the windows out facing in that direction. In the meantime, we also rang home to say that we were okay; we didn't want them to hear the news and worry about us. After this episode, the so-called Ring of Steel was formed around the City. That made us feel a little safer but played havoc with our time schedules.

Over the years we had gotten used to bomb threats, as we were forever having to evacuate buildings for suspect packages or the like and, being in a white van, we were forever being stopped—not just at the ring of steel, but by the roving patrols. On one warm sunny Saturday morning, we were pulled over and the policeman had his gun through the open driver's window asking the usual questions, and I was obviously facing him when I sensed something behind me. I turned round only to bang my face into the barrel of the gun, which was through my window. He apologised, but like I say, we never minded the security, except for one over-zealous security guard at the Union Bank of Switzerland. Whenever we drove into a car park, the vehicle would be searched and inspected underneath. At UBS we would then drive into the underground car park and ring the bell at their park gates and talk to security, and once they ascertained who we were, the gates would open and we would park up. On this one occasion, we had been working there on the Saturday, and when working in sensitive areas, we would have the company of a security guard. When we arrived on the Sunday to continue our work, we arrived at the underground car park gates, and the security guard who had spent the whole of the previous day with us was there to greet us. You would think that he had never seen us in his life before; first, he wouldn't open the gates and wanted verification that we were who we claimed to be. I thought he was joking, but no. We showed him our passes from the day before, and he rang the desk to make sure that we were booked in. In spite of the fact that our tee shirts and sweaters were emblazoned with our company name, as was our van, it took us half an hour to convince him, and then we had to spend the rest of the day with him.

It was a few years later that we were nominated as contractor to carry out some modifications, including the installation of some of our sensors on one of the floors of Lehman Bros which was being let to Natwest. By this time, my son had gone his own way, as he decided that he was getting too old for all of this running around, so I now worked mainly on my own. After the job was completed, I rang the project manager to check that everything was in order. He said it was, and that in fact ours was the only part of the contract that had gone smoothly. He was very impressed and promised that I would get a look in any future contracts that he was involved in.

It wasn't long before the first order came in—supply only, which suited me. I didn't hear any more from that job until the next order came in. An order would come in every two to three months, and this went on for a couple of years until one day I had a phone call from the site where the sensors were being installed. The guy said that I'd gotten a problem, as none of our sensors were working, and I had better get down there and sort it out. As I'd never had a problem with the equipment before and I personally tested each sensor before it was despatched, I was pretty sure that it wasn't my problem at all, but as usual this was London and it was never their problem.

I did say that I was willing to attend site the following day, provided that he give me an order number. If it was my fault, I would do the work for free, but if it wasn't, somebody would need to pay me. He agreed, as the job was due for hand over the following Monday and this was Wednesday. I took ten spare sensors just in case, and on arrival on site, I asked him to take me to the area where the sensors had been installed. I looked at the first one, and pointed out that it wasn't working because someone had painted over the lens. The next had its lens broken, and another was flashing on and off, indicating that it had been wired incorrectly. The guy apologised and asked, as I was now being paid, if I would go through the whole building and give him a report on what was required to rectify the problem. On completion, I reported to him and explained that a number of them had been painted over, some were damaged, and others had been wired incorrectly but would still function if they were rewired. Others were unable to be diagnosed, as they had also been wired incorrectly, but had been flashing for so long that either the relays or the light fitting had burnt out, or even both. I had also written this down and had had it photo copied. I told him that I had brought ten spares with me that he could purchase, but that he also needed another fifty pieces. He gave me an order for the lot and asked if I could arrange delivery for the following day so that the work could be done over the weekend before the hand over to the client. I told him that the only way I could guarantee that was to have them delivered by taxi; he agreed to pay, apologised again, and thanked me very much. I did as I promised and rang him on Monday, but got no reply, I tried a couple of times again on Tuesday with the same result, and assumed that everything must have gone according to plan. Wednesday he called me; he had been moved to his next job at Canary Wharf, but had had a call from the new guy who had taken over the finishing off. The client had moved in as planned on the Monday, but apparently our equipment was still not working. Would I again visit the site? I suggested the same terms as before, and he gave me an order number. I arrived on site with another ten spares but no one wanted to know me as it was their tea break, and I wasn't offered a cup. Shortly afterwards, the suit turned up and he was told that I was the guy who had come to fix the sensors. He turned on me, raving and shouting what a load of crap my company had supplied, and that my governor had told him that I was not to leave the site until I had gotten everything working. I just sat there and took it, apart from asking the name of the person with whom he had spoken. He couldn't remember. Once he had calmed down, I suggested that we take a look at these offending articles. He took me to the first one; the ceiling tile was still out, and my sensor was plugged in hanging there, and the lights were flashing on and off. I asked him if he had a copy of the report that I had left, and he did. I produced mine from my brief case, and I asked him if he could read, which he took offence at. I then pointed out that the report stated that this sensor had been incorrectly connected and I explained that no matter how many you plug in, they will all behave the same until the wiring is corrected. I asked to see the next problem, but it seemed that this was as far as they had gotten. His attitude changed, and I suggested that he give me one of his men so that I could work with him and show him what needed to be done. I asked to be supplied with the replacement sensors, but they had lost the fifty delivered by taxi, so we were left with the ten that I had brought with me on my first visit and the ten that I had brought on this occasion. Oh and could he find out the name of the person with whom he had spoken? We started working from the top of the building, and two floors down we were out of replacements, just as we bumped into the suit again. He asked how we were getting on, and I told him that his man was now competent enough to rectify the remaining problems. We had run out of replacements, and I asked if he wanted me to arrange another delivery by taxi. Meanwhile, his man could carry on rectifying the wiring problems. Once he had given me the order, I asked him if he had found out the name of the person with whom he had spoken. (I've been here before, remember.) He must have rung the guy then, based at Canary Wharf. "Rick Harris," he said. "Did this Rick Harris tell you whom he was sending?" I asked. "No." "So you don't know who I am?" "No." "I'm Rick Harris, and until today you and I have never spoken to each other; you have slagged my company off for no reason and put the reputation of my company on the line; when I get back, I will speak to your governor and let him know that I have never come across such a disgusting installation or such incompetence of whomever is responsible."

He was not a happy man. I was, as I had had the last laugh, and also had been paid for the equipment three times over plus two days of labour.

I did speak to his boss, who was the guy that regularly sent me orders. He asked me to send him a full report, and two weeks later I got another order from him.

TRAIN TRAVEL

During my travels on the train to and from London, and at times on the tube, I had many confrontations with what I would describe as inconsiderate passengers. Here are a few:

The first was not so much a confrontation as a frustration. I was on the tube, packed in like sardines, and a girl stood to give her seat to a lady who was obviously pregnant. Before the pregnant lady could sit down, a man had slipped into the seat instead. I was too far away to hear what was said, but he didn't give up the seat.

Many times I would point out to a smoking passenger that we were in a no-smoking compartment; most would apologise and extinguish, but some would become quite verbal. On one occasion, I was travelling with my son and with two other guys whom we had met travelling previously on many occasions. One of them decided to light up. I asked why he had decided to smoke in a no-smoking compartment; why not go into a smoking compartment? "Because my mate doesn't smoke," was his answer. It became quite heated, and I had to drag my son off of him.

Personal stereos were another pain; they wouldn't have been if they had been kept personal, but to have to listen to someone else's second-hand music was most annoying to me, especially if they were sitting next to me and I was being blasted out whilst trying to read. Once again, most were reasonable, and would apologise and reduce the volume, but not all of them were reasonable.

I was on my own sitting in the middle of the compartment, and I could hear a 'Personal Stereo'; the offender was sitting at the far end of the compartment next to an elderly gentleman. I walked down and asked him if he would mind turning down the volume. He had difficulty hearing me, so I took off his head phones and repeated my request. He told me to f*** off. I asked him to consider other passengers, especially the gent sitting next to him, who then said he wasn't happy either. He told me to f*** off again, so I returned to my seat. I then removed my snips from my tool case and sat for a while before approaching him again. Once again, I made my request and got the same response, so I cut through his headphones cable with my snips and returned to my seat. As I walked away, he shouted after me that he would report me to the conductor when he came round; there were a few cheers and he didn't report me, but for most of the rest of the journey we just glared at each other.

On another occasion, I was travelling back from London with Mike, a big lad who worked for me. It was quite a peaceful trip until we got to Coventry. Four young lads got on the train, one of them carrying a ghetto blaster, which was at full volume, on his shoulder. They sat a few seats behind us, I gave them a couple of minutes, then asked them to turn it off—and got, in return, the usual mouthful of abuse. I grabbed the set, removed the batteries, and returned the set to him. I was about to say that I would return the batteries when I got off, but I saw him dive into his large bag. Thinking that he might be going for a knife, I struggled with him to get the bag off him; when I did, I found it to be full of batteries. Mike was standing by in case the rest of them also turned on me. By this time, we had arrived at Birmingham International, and I returned to my seat and continued to read my book. I didn't notice the commotion behind me until I was confronted by a policeman and the ghetto blaster owner yelling, "That's him," pointing at me. The policeman asked him to be quiet whilst he heard my side of the story, which I relayed to him. He then ushered the lad off the train, and the train at last got under way. Apparently, as the passengers were leaving the train, one of them had reported a scuffle; hence, the intervention of the policeman. As we were leaving the train at Birmingham New Street, the station announcer was explaining that the late arrival of our train was "due to an incident at Birmingham International."

Our projects in London were widely spread over the city; deciding which tube line I would be travelling on depended on which station was nearest to the project. Most days I would get the Northern or Victoria lines from Euston station, and possibly change to another line like District or Central. If I needed the Circle, Hammersmith, or Metropolitan lines, I would walk the few hundred yards along the road to Euston Square tube station.

On arriving at Euston station one morning, I walked over the concourse down the escalator to the tube station. As I was walking down the escalator, I passed a rather large West Indian who was unwrapping his Mars bar and discarding the wrapper onto the moving stair. As I passed him, I said, "We do have rubbish bins for that you know." When I got to the bottom, I realized that

I should have gone out to Euston Square for the Circle Line, so I turned round and headed back towards the escalators and was confronted by the guy who had dropped his Mars wrapper. He was about a foot taller than I and twice as wide, and he looked down on me and said, "Just because there's police about man, don't think you're safe. I can still beat the shit out of ya." I stared back and said, "And you think I'm just gonna stand here and let you." Then walked quickly on, up the escalator, and sighed with relief when I realized that he hadn't followed me. My colleagues who had witnessed some of my escapades were always advising me to take a step back before someone did pull a knife on me or worse. I would probably now think twice, but I'm sure there is still a point where I would intervene. In fact, a more recent incident was during the foot and mouth outbreak. We were very restricted regarding where we could walk the dog; one place we were allowed was in Kington Park. Carol and I had walked Blue, and he had been swimming in the river. On our way back to the car, I spotted two older lads in the children's play area; they had lined up some glass bottles and were throwing stones at them, and at least one had already been broken. I called them over and asked what they thought they were doing, asking questions like, "Do you have younger brothers or sisters who might play here, or do you not think it stupid that you may cause injury to other toddlers or children?" The larger one of them started giving me some abuse and made the mistake of putting his face close to mine whilst telling me to "F***off grandad." I grabbed him by the scruff of his neck and pulled him even closer. He said "If you don't let go of me, I'll report you to the police." "Not if you're F****** dead, you won't." I said, then pushed him to the ground. His mate, who had just stood there with his mouth open, suggested that they clean up, and I left them to it.

PROBLEM CONTRACTS

Although I still had a few maintenance contracts from the original systems, most of them were coming to the end of their life, and maintaining most of them became more of a liability. Trying to get them to spend money on a new system was getting more and more difficult. One company near Tower Hill Docklands Light Railway Station had decided a few years previously to dispense with my services and maintain the system themselves. Then they sold the building to a French bank the owners of which realized that the system was not functioning correctly; in fact, most of the lighting never switched off. I was asked to visit the site to quote for the refurbishment of the old system or replace it with mine. I travelled to London by train and spent two days testing and writing my report and subsequently submitted quotations for both projects. After a couple of weeks, having not had a reply, I rang and asked what the situation was. I was told that it had been put on the back burner.

Twelve months later, a new man on the job rang and asked me to revisit and re-quote once again for both options. I did suggest that I just add 10 percent, but was told that even more of the system didn't function, and that so much lighting was on twenty-four hours a day that it was costing a fortune. He said that something had to be done, so once again I visited site and checked the system and duly re-quoted. Two weeks later, same reply as before, "Not yet."

The following year, I had yet another request from another new man on the job; this one I knew from another company which he had left to take on this one. I explained that I couldn't afford to keep travelling and spending so much time on site at my expense, and suggested that they pay me for my services. Then, if they went ahead with the project, I would discount these charges from the contract price. He agreed, but would have to have it sanctioned by higher authority. The higher authority wouldn't agree, so I asked him to not call again unless it was to place an order.

I'd also been involved with another company in Blechley in which I had already made a visit to survey and quote for an installation, and they wanted me to return to consider alternative methods. I decided that they wanted to pick my brains for no payment and declined.

Also around this time, I had an enquiry from the MOD and attended a meeting in Grantham where I also gave a demonstration of my products.

They seemed very impressed, but as the project had space restrictions in the ceiling void, they asked if I could overcome this problem. I said I would look at redesigning the sensor and get back to them. They also asked for a lot of other information which I had to collate, in addition to taking photographs and putting them on disc to despatch to them on the Monday, in order for them to view them on Tuesday. This was on the previous Friday. It took most of the weekend, but as the contract was worth over a million pounds, I thought it was worthwhile. I then arranged for drawings of the modified sensor to be sent to them for approval, and they asked me to attend another meeting in Grantham. At the meeting, I was grilled once again and told that it looked good on paper—but when could they see the finished article? I explained that there were a lot of costs involved in producing the modified item, and that unless I had confirmation that I had the contract, I had no intention of spending that kind of money, as it would only apply to this contract. I did offer a prototype that I could manufacture, but it would not be a working model. This was accepted and off I went and produced this mock up and returned for another meeting. Once again, they seemed impressed and thanked me for my co-operation, and a few days later I rang to find out how I stood. Apparently, I had been nominated as the supplier. I then asked how long it would be before the project started, and was told that no date had been set. They asked if I would ring a week later when they would have more information. I explained that I needed at least six weeks lead time to allow for the new circuit boards and housings to be manufactured. I rang the following week and the week after, and on the third week, I was informed that the whole project had now been abandoned. Thanks very much.

I had no plans of retiring. I always said that one day I would decide that I had had enough and would cease trading. I came very close to doing so on that day, but another small order came in that inspired me to carry on.

Shortly afterwards, I had another enquiry from the MOD, this time for a project at Faslane on the Gareloch, my old submarine base. Once again, this was going to be worth about a million. I supplied all of the information requested and also samples, which got the usual favourable reviews—and I waited.

Meantime, another MOD enquiry came in, this time from the naval base at Devonport. They had had sample waterless urinals fitted, which they were impressed with to some degree, but decided they would be better with a certain amount of occasional flushing. As we were also suppliers of urinal flushing controls, I was invited to a meeting at the naval base and was asked to design something to suit their needs. I was beginning to feel a little nostalgic, being involved in two of my old bases, even though they had changed beyond recognition since I had last visited. I sent drawings of the proposed unit with instructions on how it would operate. If successful, I was told that this would be installed in all MOD establishments. I did hear that it was successful, but it was never taken up, and neither was the Faslane project. If I had been told that we had lost the contract in each case because we were too highly priced, I could understand and possibly would have done something about it. However, to put in all of that time, expense, and effort to find that it was just an exercise on their part was soul destroying. At this time, I had about six projects quoted for, all looking favourable, and I was sure that I would get at least one. Then as they started to fold, none because of price, I was getting close to calling it a day.

I drove to London on a Saturday morning to carry out the maintenance at Barclays, Royal Mint Court, right opposite the Tower of London. I'd been maintaining this building since it was built fifteen years previously. I knew London pretty well, but I don't think I was ever able to travel the same route twice by road, as Saturday was diversion day and this Saturday was no different. The problem was that once diverted, you are never directed back onto your original route in London.

Driving along this strange road, I knew roughly where I was and that I needed to turn right. Traffic lights ahead, plenty of traffic about, can I turn right? Lights are red and I join the queue. There is a "No Left Turn" sign on the left hand traffic light but no "No Right Turn" to be seen, and the Mercedes sports car in front of me turns right and I follow. We were both pulled over by a policeman; the driver of the Merc was a very smart lady. We were asked if we knew why we had been stopped. I suggested 'security' as I had been stopped on numerous occasions previously, and the lady agreed. Then the policeman turned and pointed so they both had their backs to me, and with the noise of the traffic I couldn't hear what was said. When they turned back so I could hear, the policeman said, "See you in court."

The lady replied, "I'm F***** annoyed."

Policeman: "Don't swear at me."

Lady: " I'm not swearing at you; I'm telling you how I feel. In fact, I'm not F****** annoyed; I'm F****** furious."

I asked what the question had been, and he once again pointed at a white arrow on a blue background and asked what it meant.

I replied, "One way only."

"That's right," he said. "So why did you turn right?"

"Because there was no sign saying that I couldn't."

"But there is," he said "It's painted on the road."

"How am I supposed to see that with traffic standing on it?" I asked.

" Not my problem Sir, I'm only doing my job."

"Why is there a 'No Left Turn' sign attached to the one traffic light then?"

"Because vehicles were turning left, Sir."

"In that case then, do you not think it time that a similar sign was posted to deter people from turning right?"

"Not my department, Sir."

"Why has that van been stopped?

"Because he also turned right, Sir."

"This sounds like entrapment to me."

"Can I now take both of your details, please, and view your licences if you have them?"

"Mine's in the car," I said, and waited whilst he took the lady's details.

"Name?"

Given.

"Address?"

Given.

"Occupation?"

"Barrister."

The poor guy nearly dropped his note book. After he composed himself, he asked me to get my licence from my car and proceeded to take my details. He then asked us to wait whilst he had a word with his colleague. When he returned, he said, "I'm not going to book you on this occasion, but wait until that van has moved off before you leave, as he has already been booked." Just then the van driver came over supposedly to chat with us, but no sooner had he opened his mouth when the Bobby said to him, "If you don't move your van immediately, Sir, I'll have to book you for illegal parking." Shortly afterwards, I drove off feeling relieved, but annoyed at the injustice. I was shortly overtaken by the lady, who honked and waved. I found my way to my site, did my day's work, and returned home late that night considering whether I should call it a day during my drive home. I had another maintenance booked in St. Albans for the following Saturday, and it was on my way home after this one that I had an idea that convinced me to call it a day.

I should convert part of my house to a Bed and Breakfast accommodation.

THE B&B

During my drive home, I planned in my head how I could make the necessary alterations. On arriving home, I discussed them with Carol, who wasn't feeling too well and didn't show much enthusiasm. The following morning, I measured up and decided that my plans were feasible and started work on the alterations. I converted half of my workshop into an office and small workshop. My original office, which took up a third of the ground floor 30 feet by 20 feet extension I converted to an en-suite twin bedroom. The remainder of the extension I divided in two, one part into a double en-suite, and the other into a breakfast room. The remainder of the original workshop became a sitting room / entrance lobby complete with newly fitted entrance doors. It was ideal, as we could isolate this area from the main house, leaving our guests to come and go as they pleased without disturbing us or Carol's parents.

I carried on trading for a while just to get rid of my remaining stock; once that was gone, I removed the Web site and e-mail address and got rid of the telephone number. I now could not be contacted, so I wouldn't be tempted to get involved again if any interesting enquiries came my way.

The B&B business was quite successful, and for the most part we enjoyed it. Our guests were from all over the world, ranging from Canada, Germany, New Zealand, Russia, Georgia, China, and four groups of people from Japan, most surprising for a B&B situated in a small village in rural Herefordshire. We have many happy memories of some of our guests; one that stands out was more comical than happy:

We had two separate couples booked in for a weekend, coming from different parts of the country. The first couple arrived up the long drive, and as I was greeting them, the other couple arrived using the short drive. It wasn't until this moment that I found out that the couples knew each other, but obviously hadn't seen each other for a while, as they then ignored my efforts to get them booked in. After waiting a couple of minutes I decided to clap my hands to gain attention, and suggested that if they wanted to stay, they needed to get booked in, which we then proceeded to do. Both couples were in their thirties and considered themselves too highly placed in the world to converse with us, one lady in particular. The following morning was beautifully warm and sunny. After serving them their breakfast, I was working in the side garden and walked around to the front to see lady posh taking photographs of the house. At the same time, I saw Blue, the dog, nip into her room through the patio door that she had left open. I naturally called to him to get out; by this time, lady posh and I were at the open patio door, and lady posh said not to worry as she liked dogs. Just then Blue emerged through the opening with a pair of her knickers in his mouth, which I had to retrieve for her. It did seem to bring her down to earth.

JULIE

As a child, Julie was very quiet; even her German language teacher commented on the fact that her written work was excellent, but that she couldn't convince Julie that it was also a spoken language. Once Julie got to know you, she was a little more verbal and could be very witty and comical.

She must have had something about her, as whilst attending her grandparents' Golden wedding anniversary she found out that not many of the guests liked icing on their cake, so set up stall outside the house selling the icing. After moving in with me, we discovered that we had far too many frogs and too much frog spawn in the pond, and transported some to a nearby lake. On returning home, she made some posters and attached them to the lamp posts along the road advertising, 'Frogs and Frog spawn for sale.' Someone who was starting a wild life garden spotted the advert, and she made a lot of pocket money. She also tried the same with two arm chairs that she heard us saying we were going to sell.

When we moved to Herefordshire, she moved to Lady Hawkins school in Kington. She was now fourteen. Unfortunately, although the curriculum was the same, it was almost in reverse order to that of her previous school. She had already learnt what she was now being taught again and would obviously miss what they had already been taught, so it was agreed that she would stay with her father during the school week so that she could continue at her old school, and she would spend the weekends and holidays with us.

The arrangement didn't last very long, as in the September following her 15th birthday she became very ill and spent a lot of the next few months in the hospital for investigative tests. In the following July 1995, she was diagnosed with ulcerative colitis, and once again she was in and out of the hospital as steroids were used to try and control it. However, when the weaning off period came to the lower end of 4 mg, it would flare up again and she would be rushed back to the hospital to be intravenously fed with steroids of 30 mg. Then would start the weaning off procedure until she reached the lower dosage again. During this time, she suffered with terrible diarrhoea as part of the symptoms; she could never be more than a few seconds from a toilet. The worst case scenario, I had to move my work to the lounge and have Julie just in front of me kneeling over a pouf, as it was too painful for her to sit. This was so that I could be in constant attendance. She would shout, and I would drop everything, pick her up, and rush to the bathroom. Then I would set her on the toilet and hold her hand as she screamed with the pain, then would move her to the bidet and wash her the best we could. We couldn't use a towel to dry her, however, as it was so painful, so we used a hair dryer instead. Take her back to the lounge, and usually 20–30 minutes later we would go through the whole procedure again. This would go on day and night until she would be treated with the high doses of steroids again. This went on until October '95, when she was taken to the hospital to have her large bowel removed due to the severity of the disease. In reality, it was a life-saving operation. My son, who had shown no compassion or support until now, made the comment, "I suppose life will revolve around Julie now." Even then we didn't get any support. Not once through all of her illness did he go to see her, even to give us a break. I even had to ask him to send her a card. His callousness upset me, and I have never forgiven him.

We were very fortunate to have one of the country's top bowel surgeons at the county hospital. He explained to us that she would at first be fitted with an Ileostomy pouch connected externally to the small bowel, which would have to be emptied and changed regularly. Once she had recovered enough, she would then return to the hospital for further surgery, to have an internal pouch formed from part of her small bowel and then reconnected to her rectum, making the external pouch redundant. She returned to the hospital in March '96, and was deemed still too poorly to have more surgery. The next phase was eventually carried out in May '96 when the J pouch was formed from part of her small bowel, leaving a loop Ileostomy still connected to the external pouch. Once again, this was to give the surgery a chance to heal before the internal pouch would be used. It was July '96 that what we hoped to be the final surgery was performed to close the Ileostomy, and now she would use the internal pouch and, to all intents and purposes, would perform normally.

By this time, of course, she should have sat her GCSEs , left school and should be at university or college. However, as she hadn't been fit enough, she had missed out on her final year and was assessed for her grades.

As it looked like the operations had been successful and she seemed to be on the road to recovery, she celebrated her sixteenth birthday and signed up for the animal welfare course at Herefords Agricultural college starting in September, with the long term view of training for veterinary nurse. She was suffering a lot of pain but was determined to attend college. Each morning we would wire her up to a TENS unit before driving her to the bus, 2 miles away for her, then a 15-mile bus ride to Hereford where she would change buses for the onward journey of about 3 miles to Home Lacy. I would then meet her at the bus stop when she returned on the evening.

She lasted about six weeks before she once again became very ill, and she didn't enjoy the Christmas of '96. New Year's Eve came and she wasn't well; we'd sat with her all day and the doctor had also been to see her. By late evening, she had fallen asleep, and her Nan Maud suggested that Carol and I go to the village hall party for a break, as it was also my birthday. I took my mobile phone just in case, and just after midnight it rang. Julie had taken a turn for the worse, so we ran the 200 yards home and called the doctor; he came straight out and called for an ambulance. I stayed at home for Maud and Tom while Carol went to the hospital with Julie. I drove to the hospital the following morning to meet Carol and learnt that Julie was about to go to theatre to have one of her ovaries and fallopian tubes removed. Shortly after, she was allowed home, but she was confined to bed and the nurse visited daily. I used to tend to her dressings and other needs, and we noticed that her wound had opened and that remnants of her dinner were flowing from it as well as from other orifices. The nurse called the doctor, and she was diagnosed with fistulas in addition to the fissures that she had also developed, along with an abscess. She was once again admitted to the hospital and had the loop ileostomy restored and the abscess drained. All of this took place over January, February, and March.

With the ileostomy in place, she gained weight, and her health recovered. In November, a new pouch was formed, but by the new year she was on the downhill slide again and she was sent to see a professor at the Queen Elizabeth Hospital in Birmingham for a second opinion. She was in theatre for investigative surgery, and Carol and Julie's father were in the cafeteria when a nurse informed them that the Prof wanted to see them in ward immediately. Carol thought the worst, but on meeting, the Prof suggested that although tests for Crohns had not proved positive, all of the symptoms were present and, in view of the multiple operations on bowel, pouch, fistulas excised, etc., the only way that she was going to get any quality of life was if they performed a total colectomy and left her with a permanent ileostomy. Shortly afterwards, Crohns Colitis was confirmed. She was one of the rare cases of a person having both Ulcerative Colitis and Crohns Disease, and her case notes have been used for many seminars.

Understandably, Julie was not very happy having to live with an external bag attached to her stomach and was always conscious of it. Not a pleasant experience for anyone, let alone a young lady of nineteen.

Every six months, she had to return to the hospital for a review, usually with a registrar. Having seen the registrar, on one occasion she asked to see the stoma care nurse, as she wanted advice on medical appliances. The nurse didn't recognize her as she had blossomed so much; when she realized who she was, she asked if the Prof had seen her. Julie explained that she had only attended for a review with the registrar. "Hang on," she said, "I'll see if he's free." He was, so she took Julie to see him. He didn't recognize her either at first, but was then delighted to see how well she had progressed. After some deliberation and a coded conversation with the stoma care nurse, he suggested that he may be able to do something for her, explained the procedure, and gave her a few weeks to think about it. It meant more surgery to form an internal pouch, once again from her small bowel, and a valve also from her bowel, and from then on she would use a catheter to empty the pouch. Although not ideal, it was certainly better than what she had, and she decided to go ahead with the operation, which was a success.

We do not blame the surgeon for any of the original problems; how could we? He saved her life at least once; it was just bad luck that he had had to deal with one of the most severe cases, and we appreciate all of his efforts.

Julie had had relationships, but eventually met and married Rich, a lovely fellow of whom we think the world. As I said in my speech at her wedding, "If she had picked her own ingredients and designed her perfect man, she couldn't have done a better job." She has been through hell and taken us there with her, but she has turned out to be a wonderful, thoughtful person with a lovely personality and sense of humour.

MAUD AND TOM

Tom and Maud were lovely people and, apart from Tom's ailments, were no problem. In the early days, we could cope with them quite well. They both had a good sensor of humour; Tom was very quick witted while Maud had a dry sense of humour and didn't know she was being funny most of the time. Tom would love to come and work with me in my workshop, and I would always try to find him a job to do. He would complain to Carol that I had told him that he had to work until ten o'clock. He said, "I'm not working till ten; I'll work till half nine, but not till ten." I would take him once a week to a local care home for a bath, where he was very popular as he would play the organ and get all of the inmates singing. He was very talented musically; although he couldn't read a note of music, he could play most instruments.

He was also very popular at age concern, which was held at the village hall once a week. With all of his ailments and disabilities, I don't ever recall him complaining.

Maud would make tea for all of us at 10.30 every morning and at 4 o'clock in the afternoon, and it was mostly a happy social occasion. If Julie was around and well, she would play them up and Blue would be present, usually entertaining us.

Once Carol was involved in the garden, she would not come in, and Maud would go out and call to her with hands on hips, "Come on, Carol, time you came in and fed Julie and Rick." Tom would call her, "Mrs Arms Akimbo." One time she was going through this routine and Carol lied, "If they're hungry, they can feed themselves." Shortly afterwards, Julie went down to her Nan and asked if she had anything that she could eat, just as I passed her saying that I was going to the pub to get some crisps. Maud went outside and called Carol again and really went mad at her. Little did she know that we were all winding her up; Carol had previously prepared the meal, and Julie and I had already eaten.

Maud had been asked to not answer the phone, but one day for some reason she decided she would. The call was from the Canadian High Commission asking for me. Bear in mind that the people to whom I contracted thought that I ran a large company in some large office. Maud answered, "No he's out walking the dog." Oops!

Once Julie was reasonably well, we thought that we would get our life back and start taking some long overdue holidays. What we hadn't realized during this time was how much Maud and Tom had aged and deteriorated. Tom couldn't be left on his own, and Maud was becoming too frail to look after him—and in latter years, Carol had to do everything for her mom too.

Tom had a brain condition, which was called cataplexy; it belonged to the epilepsy family. Tom described it as feeling totally paralysed for a few seconds. Although he never went unconscious, he would lose all feeling and also his speech. If he were standing, he would fall flat on his back, very often causing a head injury. If he were sitting, he would just slump; wherever he was, you just had to leave him until it had passed. These, 'turns,' as we used to call them, could happen several times a day. Sometimes he would fall in the most awkward place, such as whilst manoeuvring between wheelchair and toilet. It was very difficult to get him back up, as he was a dead weight. He was initially confined to a wheelchair for his own safety, and was in it for the last thirty years of his life. Once Carol as a child was behind him whilst going upstairs to bed when he fell downstairs, taking Carol with him. Another time he fell on the fire, again with Carol; fortunately, the fire was out. He had worked at the BSR just down the road from where they lived, and he carried a disability card as he wasn't allowed to work on machinery. Carol used to take him to work in the car (getting him into a car was a nightmare); she was allowed to walk with him through the double rubber doors, as he couldn't get through them without some help. Carol was often in plaster casts from chest to top of legs because of a back injury, but she continued to take Tom to work even though she should not have been driving. During his last few years whilst he was at home, we did get some help, half an hour in the morning and the same again in the evening. However, as time went by, they really needed 24-hour constant care, which we gave them.

We did get some respite by arranging for them to go into a care home whilst we went on holiday, but it was hard work getting them packed and organised before we could even think of getting ourselves ready. Carol couldn't really relax whilst on holiday, and we always dreaded coming home to what news would be waiting for us. We came home from one holiday and collected them from the home two days later on the Thursday before Good Friday. Tom wasn't well when we got him home, and Friday morning was a terrible time for all of us. I was outside working when Carol called me. Tom had gone to the bathroom but didn't quite manage to transfer to the toilet. He had messed himself and it was everywhere. I managed to get him into the shower where I hosed him down, stripped him, and cleaned him up, then helped Carol to clean the wheelchair so that we could dress him and set him back in his chair before cleaning the bathroom and toilet. Once sorted, Carol went back to her chores and I continued with my job outside. Half an hour later we had a repeat performance, and I could see that Carol was nearly at the end of her tether. Once back to normal again, Carol rang the home where he had been whilst we were on holiday and asked if they could take him back. It was a long-winded process, especially being Good Friday. Before they could accept him, he had to be assessed by a doctor. This was done, and Tom returned to the home for a few more days.

As time went by, we found it more and more difficult to look after them, and it was on the advice of our doctor that we agreed they should go into a care home. Our doctor had said, "If something isn't done soon, there would be four people needing help." Father-in-law adapted quite well, as he had always been a very sociable person, but he was now very weak and slept most of the time. Mother wasn't happy, which made life difficult for Carol. She would visit every day for two or three hours, and her mother wouldn't speak to her. Carol felt that she blamed her for putting her into a home.

Tom died aged ninety-five, in November after about twelve months, and Maud died fourteen months later in a hospital in January, at age ninety-three.

BUILDING PROJECT

It was shortly before Father-in-law died that we decided to try for planning permission to build two houses in the garden, as maintaining the garden and the large house was taking up all of our spare time. We didn't want to leave the village, but we wanted to downsize; there was nothing in the village suitable, so we took this route. We were originally going to build both houses and move into one and sell the other, along with the original house. However, with all of the hassle from neighbours over our plans, we decided to build the one we wished to move into and sell the other plot and let someone else have the hassle. Our nearest neighbour gave us the most grief. One morning whilst digging out the footings, he came round and gave myself and the digger driver some verbal abuse, then tipped over the table with the drawings on it and stormed off. A week or so later he started throwing bottles and rocks over the hedge at the workmen. One of them who had a near miss wanted to go round and sort him out, but I said I would report the incident to the police instead. He with other neighbours had objected to everything we proposed, and we had a long, drawn-out battle that not only delayed the building but cost us a lot financially. His final act was to report the fact that the house was not built in exactly the right place; it appears that as the ground workers were squaring up for the foundations, they moved the one corner nearest his property closer by two or three centimetres. I think he thought that we would be made to pull the house down and start again, but all we had to do was apply for a minor amendment. When we were finalising the sale of the other plot, I learnt that I actually owned part of the drive that was the access to their property. I couldn't stop them from using it, as they had a right of way as I did over the rest of the drive. When we moved into the village, there was no mains sewerage, but the mains were being installed. We ran our own drains down the front drive, picking up the two bungalows in front of us on the way before connecting to the main sewer at the bottom of the drive. I now learnt that our awkward neighbour had run his drain through the part of the other drive that I owned. I wrote the following letter:

Firstly I apologise for any inconvenience our building project may have caused you.

Some years ago, Sheila Finlayson rang me to say that my water main, which ran through her garden, was leaking and bubbling up through the soil. I hired a man with a digger and spent the morning with him digging for the said pipe. During which time I had rang the water board, as the road had recently been tarmacked, covering the stop cocks. Shortly after we found the rupture in the pipe, the water board engineer turned up. By isolating various stop cocks, we discovered that it was not my pipe but yours. I informed your wife of the situation, who indicated that it was not her problem, but we still went ahead and repaired it and made good Mrs Finlayson's garden. My costs were £150 for the hire of the man and digger plus the best part of a day of my time. I never received a thank you from you or your wife, let alone compensation.

We looked after you daughter whilst she was ill and off school so that you could both go to work.

I allowed you to use part of my land so that you could get access around your bungalow, for which I never received thanks. All in all I think I have been a reasonable neighbour.

You have run your drains across my land without my permission.

Taking the above into consideration and the fact that all I have had from you as thanks is verbal and physical abuse.

If you were in my position having a digger on site, what would you do about those drains?

I never did get a reply, but a week later their house was on the market and they moved out shortly afterwards. We still see their three daughters and get on well with them, as we always did. We used to send a Christmas card to the family, but we only ever got one back from the girls.

The rest of the neighbours are back on friendly terms, except one that still won't speak. She now finds herself in an awkward situation, as she has to sell her house, which needs to be demolished, and she is applying for planning permission to build two semis. If this is granted, she will obviously be better off selling two building plots than selling a house that needs a lot of money spending on it. If she had stayed on friendly terms, I may have allowed access up my drive, giving the opportunity to build two detached houses instead of two small semis, which would have made her even better off. I don't think I will be objecting to her plans, as I will be glad to be rid of the eyesore of a property and possibly the overgrown fir trees, which blight the landscape.

The trouble was that a lot of our garden was not on view to us from the house, and the neighbours got the benefit of my labours in keeping it looking good, and they resented that loss.

By this time, our own house was completed, and we moved there in June 2006. We were and still are delighted with the result.

BENIDORM

During the late summer of 2008, we booked a holiday with two of our friends to spend nearly five weeks at the beginning of 2009 in Spain.

The holiday was great; we all thoroughly enjoyed it—but even that wasn't without incident. When we joined the coach for our three-day journey, a couple of the passengers already seated seemed to be doing a lot of coughing, and this was passed to most other travellers, including the two other coach loads of passengers during the four-week stay at the hotel. Two passengers on another coach didn't make the destination as they ended up in the hospital after our second overnight stop in Callela. They flew back home shortly afterwards; seven others were admitted to the hospital during their stay, one of them for most of the holiday, and one had to overstay. He was still in the hospital and too ill to travel, so he was to fly home two days later.

After about two weeks, we had been out during the evening and on our walk back to the hotel at 9.30 when we heard two explosions. Both Carol and I thought, "Terrorists" while our two friends thought it was fireworks. Shortly afterwards, two men came running towards us. I was now convinced. As they approached, they split up, and the shorter one of the two got into a car. I decided to get the license plate number and, walking in the direction of the car, I got a look at the other runner, a tall North African looking guy. I was afraid of making too obvious what I was doing, as I didn't feel like dying that night, but I got most of the number and memorised it. Carol meantime also got a good look at the tall runner. We didn't get a look at the shorter one.

Once back at the hotel, we joined in with the nightly entertainment, and the following morning at breakfast one of the other guests asked if I had heard that Joyce had been mugged the previous night. Apparently Joyce, an eighty-year-old lady, had been walking back to the hotel with her friend Juliet when she was attacked, just a few yards from the hotel. I asked what time this was and he said

9.15. So I decided to speak to her myself. I then discovered that she had had all of her money and jewellery stolen, which was in her bag that she had been clutching close to her chest. She had also suffered a lot of bruising, mainly to her chest and neck, as she had been pushed to the ground and held down by her neck whilst her bag was ripped from her. I asked her what time this took place, and she said it was around 9.15. I asked her if she had heard the explosions, and she had, just a few seconds before the attack. She said that the one guy was very tall and the other much shorter; this now convinced me that her timing was wrong and that the men whom we had seen the night before were nothing to do with the explosions but were the perpetrators of her attack. She told me that it had been reported to the police and that they were sending a taxi for her that morning to take her and her friend to the police station to give statements. I offered to write a report on our experience of the night, which I did, giving all of our details and contact numbers, etc. She passed this to the police, and they then asked if we would visit the station to look at mug shots with Joyce and Juliet. On our visit, we were not kept waiting, and met with the detective involved as well as a female interpreter. We were asked to browse through photographs on a computer, and Carol and I picked two pictures that could have been one of the assailants. We were then asked to look through photograph albums with different pictures that were mostly black and white. We once again picked two possible candidates. Afterwards, we were told that we had picked the same two on both occasions. I asked what was happening with regards to the registration number that I had given, and it was still being followed up. We were all thanked very much for our co-operation and told that hopefully we would not need to be further involved, but they had our contact details if needed. We heard no more. I suppose that if enough evidence was available without our further help, they wouldn't want the expense of flying and accommodating four people from the UK. I asked about the explosions, but they were apparently fire crackers.

Later in the week, we had arranged to go to a theatre with friends who lived in Benidorm, and the day in question was very windy. During the afternoon, Carol decided that she needed to visit the pharmacy, which was a ten-minute walk away. Once outside, it was much windier than we realized, and on turning a corner we could hardly stand. We were bent almost horizontal fighting our way forward. A lady coming the other way was being blown by the wind and was hanging onto a tree. She would let go and shoot forward to throw her arms around a lamp post, and that is how she progressed up the road. The force of the wind had blown some of the hoardings down, and many of the plastic signs were now broken and flying around with all other bits of debris, including chairs and tables blown from hotel balconies. We also passed a shop that had its glass front blown in. We returned to the hotel in much the same way as the lady whom we had previously seen travelling in that direction. Later we discovered that we had been out in 100 mph winds. The show was cancelled.

On that same evening, we could see from the hotel restaurant that there was a fire in the local mountains, and we could see it spreading, driven by the wind. The following day, we learned that a pylon had been blown down, which was what started the fire. A school and four houses were burnt down, and 14,000 people had been evacuated.

Since we didn't get to see our friends the previous night, they rang during the morning and, as the wind had subsided somewhat, they suggested picking us up and going for lunch. After lunch, they dropped us off at the hotel. As Carol left the car, she looked up at the hotel and spotted a set of patio doors hanging over one of the balconies. We rushed in to inform reception, and maintenance was called. Fortunately, they knew about it and had tied them to the rails to stop them from being blown over. They had been blown out during the previous night's wind.

CAROL

After Carol and Julie moved in with me, I bought Carol's ex husband John's share of their house and we rented the house out. Over the years, we had a variety of tenants, some good, some bad. The last one, a young girl on social security with a child, had been there for about two years when we decided to sell. As she didn't want to move, she would tell all sorts of tales to put potential buyers off, and we had difficulty removing her when we eventually did sell. Even then I tried to be helpful; she rang me to ask if she could leave her three-piece suite in the garage for a day, as she couldn't get it in the removal van. I agreed, but it was still there after a few of days, and to take it to the tip would cost me, so I asked the agents if they had her new address. They did, so I suggested that as I was having to pay for the removal of the suite, they could deliver it to her, and if she wasn't in, to leave it in the garden. It was left in the garden.

At home we were having problems with the herons taking the fish from the pond, so I suggested that we net the pond. It was winter time and it was a cold, wet day, so we were dressed accordingly—Carol with her large, warm, wax jacket. I organised the net and some long rods to thread through, and I stood on one side of the pond and Carol the other, and Julie looked on. Working our way from the narrow end to the wide end, with the last but one rod to thread, Carol leant too far out and ended up in the pond. We helped her out and took her indoors and stripped her. She was sitting by the radiator in her bra and pants with Julie in attendance whilst I sorted out her wet clothes. The phone rang; it was Paul from the company to which I subcontracted, wanting to speak to me. The conversation went something like the following:

"Hello Carol, can I speak to Rick?"

"Hello Paul, I've just fallen in the pond and I'm soaking wet."

"Oh have you? Can I speak to Rick?"

"Yes Paul, but I've just fallen in the pond and I'm soaking wet."

"Well, can I speak to Rick? I have a very irate customer on the other line and I need Rick to sort it."

Next she was playing us up. "I need a brandy and to be put to bed."

Once sorted, Julie disappeared to her bedroom, and shortly afterwards came down with a drawing of Carol being fished out of the pond with fish jumping from her pockets; that picture went up on the wall.

On one of our many stays at the cottage, we'd taken a chicken to cook for Sunday lunch. Carol had prepared the vegetables, and in went the chicken. It was a beautiful day, and Carol decided that whilst dinner was cooking she would sunbathe. After about an hour, I asked if the dinner was okay. Apparently everything was under control. An hour later I asked the same question and got the same reply; after another half hour I asked if she was sure that everything was under control. Doesn't time fly when you're napping? The chicken was now the size of a sparrow and inedible. I must admit that I was not pleased, but all Carol could do was laugh. My granddaughter, Sandra, didn't help by saying, "She did her best, Granddad."

Another of our better moments at the cottage—on another beautiful day we had a barbecue in the evening, with the music playing loud as we had no neighbours to worry about. We had the top off the jeep, and Julie was using this as her stage to dance on. After eating and a few drinks, Carol and I were doing a little rock and roll when I spun round, demolished the barbecue, slid under the jeep, and came out the other side still dancing. Oh what a night!

Getting ready to go on holiday, Carol decided that she was going to take her knitting. I thought that I had talked her out of it, but as David was dropping us off at the airport, he said, "Don't forget to write down everything she does so that we can fill the lads in on the train when you come back."

We checked in our baggage and were singled out for ours to be X-rayed, then through security, who found her knitting needles. A good start for a write up.

As you may have gathered, Carol is a rare character and is loved by everyone who knows her; she is full of fun and is a must at any party. There are certain people who are on her wavelength and could banter comically with her all night.

She has had and still has health problems. At the age of twenty-four, she had an accident at the hospital where she worked. She injured her back and had to endure hospital stays on traction to neck and back, followed by plaster casts and neck braces. All of this was the incorrect treatment, as was discovered later. She has also suffered from psoriasis since she was twenty. Fifteen years ago, she started suffering with complete body pain. Since that time, she has been diagnosed with and treated for, arthritis, rheumatoid arthritis, ME, and finally, during the early part of 2008, psoriatic arthritis and fibromyalgia. The latter, I think, is the name given to anything that doesn't come under any specific category. The pains sometimes last for months and she has to survive on morphine patches, and then it eventually goes into remission, which can last for a few weeks and, if lucky, a few months before it flares up again for no apparent reason.

She has also helped her mother to look after her father since she was a teenager, doing a lot of the tasks he would have done, such as wallpapering, laying carpets, gardening, etc. Because of his cataplexy, he was unable to do many tasks for fear of injuring himself. Carol had her hands full when, during latter years, she had to not only do for her dad but also for her mother, who became very frail. Hence, she also had to wash and do for her. All of this, and the traumatic experience of seeing Julie go through her dreadful suffering during her teenage years and beyond, took its toll on Carol's health. Thank goodness, they all had this marvellous sense of humour which helped us through a lot of misery and hard work. Most of the time, she has remained cheerful and always prepared to laugh at herself and make others laugh. She is a remarkable woman.

Her main employment was as secretary in a drawing office, where she also did some technical drawings (taught by the lads), and as secretary in the X-ray department at Wordsley Hospital, Stourbridge. She also worked as receptionist in the X-ray department at Russells Hall Hospital, Dudley, working late evenings and weekends.

She had a very unhappy first marriage, which after fifteen years ended in divorce.

After we had lived together for about two years, I was invited to a wedding, and when I got there, I found that I was the groom. Well it was almost like that. Carol suggested that we get married, so I suggested that she organise it all and I'd turn up, and she did. She did a wonderful job, including arranging a week of glorious weather; the day itself couldn't have gone better. The following day, we had a barbecue at home when most of the guests turned up, and we had another memorable day in more ways than one, as one of the young lads playing cricket in the bottom garden cut his leg badly and was rushed to the hospital for stitches.

We had a few outings during the week, then finished the week off with a trip to an outdoor music festival the following Saturday, which ended in a wonderful firework display to Handel's Water Music. The following day the weather broke, and we were back to a normal British summer.

We had spoken to our local vicar regarding a church wedding. When he came to visit, we learned that he was also ex Royal Navy, and we talked about some of our experiences. Then he suggested that if we wanted him to marry us, we would have to live apart for six months. We turned him down, and Carol then spoke to the Minister at the church where she had previously married, which was also where she (before she moved a little distance away to live with me) and her mother and father regularly attended. We're very grateful to Peter and his wife Jasmine not only for marrying us, but for all their help, support, and advice over the years with the funerals of five of the elder members of Carol's family and, of course, Julie's wedding.

Carol and I had gone to a conference in a hotel and, as we were early, called at the bar for a drink. Then Carol needed the loo before going upstairs to the conference room. The stairs were situated directly opposite the open double doors of the bar, which was fairly crowded. When Carol came from the toilets, I was waiting at the bottom of the stairs and we proceeded upwards. By the time we reached the first landing, a lady had caught up with us and pointed out to Carol that the back of her skirt was tucked into her knickers, giving a wonderful view to all of the occupants of the bar.

*****

Since marrying, Carol and I had tried to continue taking two foreign holidays each year. We'd visited Tenerife a few times, as well as the Gambia and also Madeira, but the most memorable was our first trip to France to visit Carol's cousin.

I booked the car ferry and decided that with all of the driving that I was doing, I didn't really want a busman's holiday, so I booked ourselves and the car onto a train for the journey from Boulogne to Brive, where the cousin would meet us and we would follow to their home near Sarlat in the Dordogne. Nearing the departure date, I had a call from the travel company saying that we could not travel by ferry on the Tuesday, but that they could find us space on the following Thursday. I said that this would be fine as long as the return journey was also altered to Thursday. The journey from home to ferry and across the channel went smoothly. We were directed to where the train was waiting, and we joined the queue to load the car onto the transporter. When things started to move, I gave Carol the travel documents and suggested that she and daughter Julie board the train and find our compartment. Shortly afterwards, I joined them where they were waving to me from the train window. It was about seven in the evening when we departed; once settled, we made our way to the restaurant car and had a meal and a couple of drinks before turning in for the night. I woke up at about seven o'clock the following morning as we were leaving Toulouse. I said to Carol that I thought Toulouse was further south than Brive and left the compartment to investigate. I got talking to a frequent English traveller and asked him about this, but all he wanted to do was talk about his previous experiences until he finally said, "Of course a lot of the passengers got off at Brive at five o'clock this morning." "That's what I've been asking you," I said, and headed for the restaurant, but could find no one who spoke English. Then someone took me to the conductor, who could speak the language better than I. He said that someone should have woken us before Brive; could he see my tickets. We made our way back to the compartment where Carol produced the tickets. "Ah, I see the problem," he said, " right compartment, wrong carriage." Unfortunately, the next stop was Narbonne, on the Mediterranean, three hours farther down the track. By this time, Cousin had found our car at Brive, but no trace of us, and had reported us missing. An alert had been put out, as people had recently been mugged and thrown from the train. The conductor said that he would report that we were found safe. We then went to investigate the compartment in which we should have travelled; it was much better, with its own wash basin and potty—first class, just as I had paid for. The conductor came to see us again before we arrived at Narbonne and said that he would be travelling back to Toulouse on the return train that we would be travelling on, and to meet him on the platform at a given time. On arrival at Narbonne, we were handed over to a PR person who arranged a telephone call to Cousin, who was still waiting at Brive and would wait for our return. We had quite a wait before our next train journey, so we had a meal just outside the station. Then we returned and found our conductor. Carol wouldn't leave his side, and once on the train, I wasn't allowed to read my book in case we missed the stop at Brive—especially as Carol had spotted "Berlin" on the front of the train.

Having left Toulouse behind for the second time that day, the new conductor asked for our tickets. Carol was digging in her bag for them until I reminded her that we didn't have any for this trip, I was trying to explain to the conductor when he smiled and said "Ah yes, my friend told me of you."

On reflection, we were treated very well by all concerned, whether that was because they felt that the fault was on their part, not noticing that we were missing from our compartment, or whether it was the fact that we kept smiling, even when others may have been giggling at our misfortune.

We eventually de trained at Brive at five o'clock on the Friday evening, twelve hours later than we were scheduled. Then we found our car and followed a frustrated but relieved cousin and family the sixty miles to their home. The next two days were most enjoyable, and included opportunities to see the many visitors who came to see the family who were 'Lost in France.'

On the Monday, we decided to arrange what we were going to do over our remaining few days, and I asked Carol for our travel documents in order to check the time of train and ferry departures. I was most upset when I realized that our return bookings had not been altered, in which case our train would be leaving that evening to catch the Tuesday morning crossing.

Whilst standing in the queue at Brive, I could hear the story being told of the family that went missing a few days previously. I had to point out that it was me. We still have many a giggle when relating this story.

We visited again the following year, but this time I drove all the way.

When I took Carol and Julie to Tenerife for the first time, I decided one day to take them to Calletta beech. We parked the car and set out on the best part of a mile walk over moonscape terrain, where the molten lava had met the sea all of those years ago. The last few yards were the most difficult, as we had to walk round a narrow ledge and duck under an overhanging rock, at the same time jumping across a chasm about three feet wide and twenty feet deep, and dodging the water spout that occasionally shot up as the waves entered the chasm. Having made it safely there and back, both Carol and Julie decided that, although it was a beautiful, secluded beach, they wouldn't be going again. The expansion of the building work undertaken in Tenerife has now completely covered this area.

When I first met Carol, she couldn't swim. In fact, I would say that she was aqua phobic, but to impress me she lay in the shallow water of the beach in the Gambia trying to swim, dragging her stomach over the sand. Suddenly she let out a scream, and, when she managed to stand up, she had a rather large crab clinging to her hand.

Carol was determined to learn to swim; she would manage half a width by the end of a swimming session, but on her next visit would need to start all over again, so she never got beyond the half width. To give her a better chance, the last few months before we moved to Herefordshire, we decided that we would join the early birds at the local pool. We did this faithfully, including Julie, who was a competent swimmer anyway.

One day after swimming, Carol couldn't get into her locker so she asked one of the female attendants for help. She couldn't get the key to open it either, so a man was called, who took about fifteen minutes to strip the door from the locker, only to find someone else's belongings in it. It was the wrong locker—Carol's locker was the one below. After that embarrassing episode, Julie refused to go again, as did Carol. I had been waiting outside all this time, oblivious to what was going on, wondering what was taking so long. We had been going for weeks, and she still hadn't gotten farther than the half width. It has only been in the last year that she has learned to swim, since we have been able to hire a private pool, where we swim once a week. But she is still reluctant to enter a pool with other people in it.

Photograph taken on Carol's 60th birthday

40. Julie and Richard's wedding

BAD NEWS WEEK

Shortly after my seventieth birthday, I was struck down with a virus, which laid me up for six weeks. It took many more weeks to recover fully, during which time I had many blood tests. Once recovered, I realized that I was now without stress; Julie was happily married, Carol was in remission from her pains, we had sold the original house, we were financially okay, and life seemed to be good. It wasn't until now that I realized that life really had been one long battle and that stress had been a major part of my life.

Later in the year, I had pains in my arms and consulted the doctor, suggesting that they may be side effects from the statins that I was taking. The doctor wasn't sure; he thought it may be from the original virus and decided to take more blood tests. I asked if it was possible to include a prostate test. He asked if I had any symptoms, which I didn't have, but knew of the possibilities for a man of my age. The blood was taken on that Tuesday. Thursday the Doctor rang and asked me to go and see him that afternoon. He later told me that my PSA was high and that he would make a hospital appointment. The following day, the hospital rang with an appointment for the following Monday. By this time, I was obviously thinking the worst, as things were moving so quickly. I was examined on the Monday, and an appointment was made for a scan and biopsy, which took place the following week. During this time, Julie and Richard had been preparing for IVF; because of Julie's earlier surgery, she wasn't expected to conceive naturally. The following week I had my biopsy, and afterwards whilst having coffee in the hospital cafeteria with Carol, I had a phone call from Julie telling us that she was pregnant. We were obviously over the moon and felt like celebrating. Two weeks later, after having a scan, she was told that a heartbeat couldn't be found but that this sometimes happened as it could be hidden. "Come back for another scan next week," they told her. The next scan result on a Monday showed that she had lost the baby. Tuesday I had to return to the hospital for the results of my biopsy. Julie commented, "We both can't have bad news." When Carol and I walked into the consulting room, the presence of a Macmillan nurse confirmed my suspicions. The consultant then informed me that I had prostate cancer. I would next have an MRI scan to see the extent of the cancer, and Cara the nurse would explain the procedure to me and would be my dedicated nurse. Although I was expecting this outcome, it still came as a shock, and Carol was devastated. A week later, Blue had a stroke; shortly afterwards, Julie miscarried.

Having recovered from all of this, I remained positive. I decided that I had to practice what I preached: my fate was out of my hands, and worrying certainly wasn't going to help; in fact, it could possibly be detrimental. Earlier in the year, before all of this started, we had booked to go on holiday to Benidorm with two of our friends for the whole of January. I explained this to Cara, and she arranged my treatment around it; first was the MRI scan, which showed that the cancer had spread to the surrounding tissue. Then came the hormone tablets and the four hormone injections at monthly intervals—the first just before our holiday, the second the day we returned, another a month later, two weeks before the Radio therapy treatment started, and the final one half way through my treatment. The treatment involved a daily minimum round trip of 124 miles travelling to Cheltenham, five days a week for eight weeks. The distance varied each day, as I was taken by a hospital car driver and we had to pick up other patients on the way. Having completed the treatment, I will be monitored for the rest of my life. During the final days of my treatment, I noticed that my left leg was swollen. I reported this to the Radio Therapists, and they suggested that I contact my GP. He suspected a DVT (Deep vein thrombosis) and sent me for a scan, which proved inconclusive. With all of the travelling and sitting while waiting for treatment that I had endured over the eight weeks, my GP thought it likely that this was the cause, and thought it wise to assume that I did have a DVT. He treated me accordingly, with daily blood-thinning injections in the stomach for three weeks, and Warfarin tablets for six months.

Life goes on, and so does the battle.